Edavalikel Philipos

The Syrian Christians of Malabar

Otherwise Called the Christians of S. Thomas

Edavalikel Philipos

The Syrian Christians of Malabar
Otherwise Called the Christians of S. Thomas

ISBN/EAN: 9783337166298

Printed in Europe, USA, Canada, Australia, Japan

Cover: Foto ©Lupo / pixelio.de

More available books at **www.hansebooks.com**

THE
SYRIAN CHRISTIANS OF MALABAR:

OTHERWISE CALLED

THE CHRISTIANS OF S. THOMAS:

BY THE

REV. EDAVALIKEL PHILIPOS,

CHOREPISCOPUS, CATHANAR OF THE GREAT CHURCH AT COTTAYAM,
IN TRAVANCORE.

EDITED BY THE

REV. G. B. HOWARD, B.A.

CHAPLAIN OF S. MARY'S HOME, STONE, NEAR DARTFORD; AUTHOR
OF "THE CHRISTIANS OF S. THOMAS AND THEIR LITURGIES;" AND
FORMERLY SCHOLAR OF S. JOHN'S COLLEGE, CAMBRIDGE.

— ◆ —

OXFORD and LONDON:
JAMES PARKER AND CO.
1869.

PREFACE BY THE EDITOR.

THE preparation of the following Treatise is due, I believe, to a hope indulged by its Author that some interest in behalf of his suffering countrymen had been awakened in this country by a work of mine published in 1864, entitled, "The Christians of S. Thomas and their Liturgies." It was sent to me more than two years ago for publication, but as no funds were sent to meet the expense, and none could be expected so far as the Author was concerned, I was unable to put it at once into the printer's hands. However, as I had promised my native friend to do what I could, and as I had led him, I fear somewhat too rashly, to expect that I should be successful in getting his work published, I have determined to issue it without further delay.

The kind reception accorded to the little work already alluded to, induces me to hope that this Treatise will meet with at least equal favour. Those who take an interest in the affairs of Oriental Churches generally will find here a sketch of the First Four General Councils (together with the Latrocinium) made from the stand-point of an Eastern Jacobite, with no inconsiderable amount of information as to the ecclesiastical observances and tenets of the Jacobites. Those again, who, whether they enter deeply or not into subjects such as the foregoing, are possessed by an earnest missionary spirit, will be able to judge how far the object of their hearts would be likely to be promoted by any steps they may have thought practicable in conjunction with the Christians of S. Thomas. And lastly, to those who yearn, above all things else, for the advancement of the Visible Reunion of Christendom, as the fulfilment of our dear Lord's most earnest prayer, and as essential to the completeness of the Church, and to her ultimate victory over evil, these pages will afford matter for deep reflection, and possibly a basis for active exertion also.

While on this subject I would beg leave to add a word or two on a question which is intimately connected with it. The "Church Review" for August 15, 1868, contained an article

advocating co-operation with the Christians of S. Thomas in
missionary work.   A similar desire led, in the early part of
the present century, to the establishment of the College at
Cottayam under the auspices of the Church Missionary Society;
but the position of that Society in regard to the native Church
has for very many years past been one of violent antagonism.
I had myself cautiously hinted at the possibility of a renewal
of our relations with this interesting Church some years ago,
(see the " Christians of S. Thomas," &c., pp. 112, 113, 171,
172,)—cautiously, because I was then to a certain extent aware
of their Jacobitism.   I was willing to hope, however, and
would fain have persuaded myself, that its members were not
consciously implicated in that heresy, and that the expressions
in their Liturgies and other services which tended in that
direction were merely the result of habitual usage.   The present Treatise, I fear, precludes us from continuing to entertain
any such hope, and—with grief I say it—I do not see how,
knowing their tenets as we now do, we could co-operate with
them, without thereby becoming partakers with them in that
heresy by which, alas, they are separated from the One Holy
Catholic and Apostolic Church of the East and West.

Liberavi animam meam!   But having felt constrained to
say thus much, I am anxious to add that I would go to meet
them to the farthest possible extent that might be consistent
with loyalty to the Church.   Hard words and harsh treatment
have ever failed to bring back wanderers from the Faith:
gentleness and love have brought back many a one.   Moreover, the contention between the Orthodox and the Jacobites,
so far as my weakness is able to apprehend its nature, is one
that none but the most profound theologians could enter into,
so deep is the Mystery concerning which the dispute arose.
Surely this consideration should make us cautious as to the
language we use in reference to these separated Churches,
even while, following the guidance of the holy Fathers, we
ourselves adhere rigidly to the teaching of the Catholic Church.

But indeed it does not seem to me an easy thing to discover
the exact nature of the question in dispute.   The language of
our Second Article might lead an Anglican to suppose that the
question lay as to the superior fitness of applying the term
UNION or CONJUNCTION to express the mysterious " concourse"—I use S. Cyril's word—of the Two Natures in the
Person of our Lord after His Incarnation.   I formerly held
this idea, and gave expression to it in the " Christians of

S. Thomas," pp. 169, 171. But I believe it is erroneous. There seems to be no special stress on the word *conjunctæ* of our Second Article : indeed, so far as the use of the term *Union* is concerned, the holy Councils and the Catholic Doctors agree with the Monophysites. S. Cyril of Alexandria continually employs the words *union, united, unification*, and expressly rejects the word σνναφεία, *conjunction*, as insufficient to express the Mystery. (See the passage quoted in my note at p. 6.) And the Council of Chalcedon itself adopts the term *Union* in the very sentence in which it anathematizes the followers of Eutychus, as those " who speak of two natures before the *Union* and feign one after the *Union*." This is not a mere quotation of terms used by the Eutychians, for, a little farther on, the Council again employs the term in the well-known passage, ἕνα καὶ τὸν αὐτὸν Χρ. " One and the Same Christ, Son, Lord, Only-begotten, to be acknowledged in two Natures, inconfusedly, unchangeably, indivisibly, inseparably, the distinction of the Natures being in no wise taken away by the *Union* (ἕνωσιν), but rather the property of each Nature being preserved," &c.

The Jacobites also—if Assemani correctly represents their teaching in what he gathers from the writings of Xenajas or Philoxenus (tom. ii. p. 25)—expressly reject the notions of conversion, confusion, commixture, or separability, in defining the mode of the Union : and, if it be so, what is there to hinder their subscribing to the Definition of the Council of Chalcedon ? It has not been my fortune to come across any exposition of the Jacobite doctrine as given by their own pens, in which these notions are each and all of them rejected, except in a letter from Cathanar Philipos to myself, dated January 6 (18), 1868. This letter is written in Syriac, and for fear I should not understand it, the writer added a compendious translation. The following is the passage I refer to :—

Literal Translation of the Cathanar's Syriac.	*The Cathanar's English.*
" And behold, concerning the Faith of the Syrians that are in Christ, I have written openly in that little book of mine (i.e. this present work) ; and now also I write concerning it.	" Although I have stated more plainly and widely about the doctrin of the Syrians in my tract which I had already forwarded to your honour, yet at present I briefly state about it in this also.
" We Syrians, then, believe	

Literal Translation of the Ca-thanar's Syriac.	*The Cathanar's English.*
that the Word of God, One of the Holy Trinity, came down from heaven, and was begotten in the Flesh of the Spirit of Holiness, and of the blessed Mary, the Virgin, the Mother of God. And He is Perfect God, and Perfect Man. And after that the Two Natures were united in Him—that is to say, the Nature of His Godhead, and the Nature of His Manhood—it cannot be that they shall be separated or divided for ever. Amen. Now Nestorius, with his heretical companions, taught that Mary the Virgin brought forth a Man, Christ. And in that Man the Divinity entered and went forth as was necessary. Wherefore Two Natures were separately in Christ, the Nature of the Godhead, and the Nature of the Manhood; as water with oil : and this is not so. "But the Syrians believe that the Nature in Christ is one : that the Two Natures were united one with another; because in Christ the Two Natures were mingled together (*ethmazeg*)—the Nature of the Godhead and (that) of the Manhood—like wine with water. And whereas it is said that there is One Nature in Christ, it is for the confirmation of the Unity of the Two Natures one with another," &c.	"We believe that the Word of God, One of the Holy Trinity, came down from heaven, and was Incarnate of the Holy Ghost, and of the blessed Virgin Marry the Mother of God. After God the Word was incarnate, *the two perfect Natures,* both Godhead and Manhood, *were joined together* in one nature, *without confusion, without mixture, without change, without devision for ever and ever* [a]. "The doctrine of Nestor, the Virgin has brought forth a person, the Christ : in the same person the Divinity will sometimes rest, and sometimes leave, as is necessary. By that, both two natures, Godhead and Manhood, as water and oil, were separately joined : this is wrong in their belief. "But the belief of the Syrians, that in Christ, the Two Natures, Godhead and Manhood, as water and wine, were joined together in one person ; and that two Natures together in one Nature. But we say of the One Nature, that the junction of Two Natures should be firm and perfect," &c. [I have given my friend's words and spelling as he wrote them.]

Here, then, we have an explanation of the sense in which

---

[a] I notice that the words I have printed in italics are exact repetitions of my own expressions in a letter I had previously sent to my friend. Only he has changed the words "in the One Person of our Lord," into "in One Nature."

the Author would illustrate the Mode of Union by the Analogy of a mingling of wine with water. It is an emphatic protest against Nestorianism.

The following extracts from the writings of Xenajas will, I think, throw some additional light on the question before us, as tending to shew that the Monophysite Doctors (among whom Xenajas was prominent) were actuated by the fear that a Quaternity might come to be acknowledged and adored instead of the Most Holy Trinity. Hence perhaps the earnestness with which they inculcated the absolute Oneness of the "Nature"—and the word in their mouths seems to be equivalent to *Person*—of our Lord Jesus Christ after the Incarnation. The original is to be seen in a Syriac MS. of venerable antiquity (the sixth or seventh century), now in the British Museum, numbered Additional MSS. 14,529.

At fol. 65 verso we have the following :—

"Again, Mar Xenaja his (Treatise) on the distinction of those heresies that are held in error.

"Mani and Marcion and Eutycha denied the embodiment of the Word of God of the holy Virgin Mary; and thought the Mysteries of the Dispensation a Spectre and a Phantom; and said that the Word passed through the Virgin as through a conduit, receiving nothing of Mary.

"Valentinus and Bardesan said that the Word sent down a body from Heaven, and that the Humanity of the Word was not from Mary.

"And Apollinaris thought that the Embodiment of God the Word was without Intelligence.

"And Eunomis said that the Word received only a Body from Mary, but did not receive a Soul. But he said that the Divinity filled the place of a Soul.

"And Diodorus, and Theodorus, and Theodoreta, and Nestorius, ... and Barsuma, said that Christ was simple Son of Man, a Man who was made illustrious by His good works; and God loved Him, and dwelt in Him, and by Him redeemed the Sons of Men; saying that He died, and He that dwelt in Him raised Him up. And they divide Him into Two Sons, and Two Natures, and into the Two Persons of God the Creator and the Son of Man the Created.

"Arius said that the Son of God was a Creature.

"Paul of Shamishatia said that Christ was simple Son of Man, like one of the Prophets and the Righteous.

"*And the addition that was made in Chalcedon speaks of a Fourth Number, and brings in the Messiah after the Trinity.*

"And the Jews say, &c. . . . .

"Orthodox Christians, Sons of the Holy Church, confess One

Nature (Chino) of the Father, and of the Son, and of the Holy Ghost ; believing that One of the Persons (Chanumo) of this Essence, medial in the Trinity, came down, and was incarnate from the Holy Ghost (and) from the Virgin Mary, and took a body from her ; though His embodiment did not make any addition to His Person (Chanumo). For the Trinity remains as it was, a Trinity. Also after He was incorporate, He was one of the Trinity, God the Word. And He was truly born, and was seen in the World, and ate and drank, and was weary, and was refreshed, and in truth tasted sufferings ; and was crucified and was buried, and rose the third day according to the Scriptures, both by the Will of His Father, and by the Will of His Holy Spirit ; and sitteth on His Eternal Throne on the right hand of His Father ; and He will come to judge the dead and the living : To Whom be glory," &c.

On fol. 68 of the same MS. we have ten sentences of Anathema against the Council of Chalcedon, from which I extract the following :—

"No. 8. And again we anathematize and set aside the Council of Chalcedon, because in the One Lord Jesus Christ, the Only-begotten Son of God, it separates the Natures and the Properties and the Actions, and the Heights and the Humiliations, and the Divinities (plur.), and the Humanities (plur.) ; and thinks of Him as Two ; and *brings in a Quaternity*, and worships the simple Son of Man ;" &c.

A similar dread of worshipping a Quaternity instead of the Trinity is shewn in the following extract from the next following leaf of the same MS. :—

"Again, responsive sentences of Mar Xenaja, when one is asked, How believest thou ?

"My Faith is in the Trinity ; and the Trinity is not defective or wanting that It should be a Duality ; and not added unto Itself, so that It should grow to a Quaternity. Not defective from Its perfection : and not receiving another Person extrinsic to Itself. Every thing extrinsic to the Trinity is a Created thing ; and whatsoever is in It is Essence, and adorable. There is not anything extrinsic to It to be adored : nor within It is aught that doth adore. . . .

"One of the Persons, therefore, of this Trinity came down from heaven by [? means] of exinanition, and of the Holy Virgin became the Son of Man, because He is God. And in His Entity—or rather, perhaps, in His *becoming* (the Son of Man)—His Nature was not changed ; and addition to His Person there was none."

Such teaching as the above does not seem, in its intention and purport at least, so far from that of the Catholic Church, as to exclude the hope that, old animosities being laid aside, the Jacobites of the present day might be induced to come to an agreement with us, especially as no new formula of Faith would have to be imposed; for as the Athanasian Creed (which would present the greatest difficulty) has never yet been adopted by any Œcumenical Council, it cannot claim any such paramount authority as would have belonged to it if it had been adopted by the Universal Church.

So long, indeed, as the Jacobites continue to anathematize the Œcumenical Council of Chalcedon, one cannot but feel that to unite with them would be an act of disloyalty, and even perhaps of *ipso facto* schism. Yet I cannot forbear expressing a hope that this need not always be. Might not some basis of a Concordat be found in the examination of the meaning of the word *Nature* as used by either side? The extracts given above furnish us with at least one instance in which the word Nature is used to signify the Eternal Essence of the Godhead; and others might be easily quoted from the language of S. Cyril. This subject is examined at some length, I think, in a most able article by Dr. Newman, published in the *Atlantis* some years ago.

It is time to return to our Author and his Treatise. It was written, he tells me, first in Malayalim, and afterwards translated into English by himself. With becoming modesty he invited me to make whatever alterations I pleased; but, as will be seen, very few have been necessary. Where there is any correction of my own it is *always* indicated by *curved* Brackets: square Brackets are such as have been introduced by the Author. This remark, however, does not apply to the spelling, in which I have taken the liberty of making a few corrections here and there without calling attention to them; such are Nicene for Nicen, Quick for Quicks, Nicæa for Nice (though to be sure that name is often spelled Nice, even among ourselves), choosing for chossing, Virgin for Vargin (repeatedly), Thirdly for Thard, Archdeacon and Subdeacon for Archdiyacaon and Hupdiyaknon, cursed for coursed, &c., some twenty-five or thirty words, I think, being all that required correction in the whole work. In the Proper Names I have seldom ventured to make any correction, feeling that the Syrian method of spelling them, where it can be properly represented by English characters, has a peculiar interest of its own.

The following is an account of the Author's family, as given by himself in one of his letters to me:—

"And again, thou askest of me, in thy letter concerning my quality, O my beloved Brother. And many priests have stood up in my family, one after another, for a long continuance of times: and they have all been irreproachable Doctors, and I am weak and simple. My Father also was a zealous Priest in the Apostolic and well-known Faith; and he performed his life in the reading and study of the Holy Scriptures, and did not at all care for anything concerning his bodily matters. And he is gone from the life of this world: and I, by the power of God, am named a Priest of the house of the Syrians of Malabar, also (of) the house of our Lord the holy Patriarch of Antioch, and (of) the house of all the Syrians in the Land of Turkey. And I am not rich in money, but I am poor and straitened. May God, Who bedeweth all flesh, bedew me also by His grace: Whom we glorify and bless for ever and ever. Amen."

In another letter he tells me that some years ago he—

"purchased a Lithographic Press, with a determination of printing all other Syriac Books except the Bible[b], and established a school for the education of ministers in the Church."

"Unfortunately," he adds, "a famine arose, such as was never before felt in this country, and being unable to carry on the works I commenced, I discontinued it with the hope of carrying my views into effect, whenever such an assistance would come as that bestowed upon the Widow of Zarephath of Zidon, through the great Prophet Elijah (1 Kings xvii. 9)."—*Letter of Dec. 17, 1866.*

Return, we beseech Thee, O God of Hosts :
Look down from heaven, and behold, and visit this Vine.

GREENHITHE,
F. of S. Barnabas, 1869.

[b] They have the Bible already, beautifully printed for them by the British and Foreign Bible Society.

P.S. July 23, 1869. I have this morning received a Letter from the Author, of which the following is the Translation:—

Glory to the Living God.

To my Brother the Priest George Howard the honoured, Curator of the House of Refuge of Saint Mary, in the city of Stone in England; from Chori Phillipos the lowly, Priest of the great Church of Cottayam in Malabar: abundant salam.

O illustrious Brother, I the weak one sent a letter to thy love on the 13th day of the month Adar (or March) in this year, and I hope it has already reached thee. And I am much surprised that I know nothing concerning the printing of my little book [I wrote to him on the 25th June to tell him about it]. And again, O my honourable Brother, I have, in the course of years, made, with much labour and abundant research, a Book concerning the History of the Syrian Church of Malabar, from the days of the holy Mar Thomas the Apostle to the present day. Besides this book of history I have other books; and I am very anxious to print these books in the language of Malabar, and in the language of England. And here there is also a Printing office for printing them, but I have no money to print them withal; and here among the Syrians there is no one who will assist me with money, because of the great disturbance that exists among us, owing to the contention and the quarrel and the divisions of the Patriarchs: and by reason hereof I am much grieved in my heart. And not this alone: I greatly fear that, if these above-mentioned books are not printed, they will be lost and destroyed after my death, and the great labour I have taken will be in vain: now therefore I have thought in my heart that there are in England good and rich men, true Christians, who will and delight and consort together in good works such as this; and that these will help me out of the abundance that God has given them, if they understand this thought of my heart. However, I do not at all know their names, so that I might write letters of entreaty to them, and petition them of their loving-kindness: wherefore I entreat of thy love, that, if this thought of my heart is pleasing, thou wilt straightway write me their names, so that I may send letters to them, and beg them to help me in my poverty. And thus know. Give salam to the priest Denton, and to the priest George Nugee, honoured Brethren, and also to thy laudable helpmate, and to thy dear children. And again I ask of thy love, not to forget me from thy heart, and not to cut off thy letters from me. And quickly send me a reply to this letter. And mayest thou remain strong in much peace. And our Lord Jesus Christ be with us for ever. Amen. It was written on the 3rd day of the month Chaziran of the Syrians, in the year 1869 of our Lord; from Cottayam.

Chori Phillipos the humble.

{ write me the names of the true }
{ Christians in English. }

On the Nature of the Syrian Church.

Q. 1. WHAT is the belief of the Syrians with regard to God?
A. They believe in the Holy Trinity [1], which is the Father, the Son, and the Holy Ghost [2], the only [3] and true God.

1. Gen. i. 26 ; and xi. 7. 2. Matt. xxviii. 19.
3. 1 Tim. ii. 5 ; Mark xii. 29, 32.

Q. 2. How do they believe in the Father?
A. They believe in Him, the Almighty Creator of heaven and earth, and of all things both visible and invisible.

Rom. xi. 36. 1 Cor. viii. 6. Eph. iii. 9.

Q. 3. How do they believe in the Son?
A. They believe Him to be the Only-begotten [1] Son of the Father, before all worlds [2], the true God [3], one equal to the Father; and that, for the salvation of Mankind, He of His own will [4] descended from Heaven, and became Man, having taken His body from the Holy Ghost [5] and from the Virgin Mary the Mother of God; and that He suffered and was crucified [6], dead [7], and buried [8], and that the third day He rose [9], and ascended to Heaven, and sat on the right hand of the Father [10], and that He cometh in great glory to judge both the quick and the dead [11].

1. John i. 14, 18.
2. Rom. xvi. 25.
   1 Cor. ii. 7.
   Eph. iii. 9.
   2 Tim. i. 9.
   Titus i. 2.
   1 Pet. i. 20.
3. Rom. ix. 5.
   Acts xx. 28.
   Heb. i. 8.
   1 John v. 20.

4. John x. 18.
   Gal. i. 4.
5. Matt. i. 10.
   Luke i. 35, 43.
6. Matt. xxvii. 35.
   Acts ii. 23.
7. Rom. v. 8.
   Rom. vi. 10.
   Rom. xiv. 15.
   1 Cor. xv. 3.
8. 1 Cor. xv. 4.

9. Matt. xxviii. 6.
   Rom. i. 4.
   1 Cor. xv. 4, 20.
10. Mark xvi. 19.
    Ps. cx. 1.
    Acts vii. 55.
11. Matt. xxv. 31.
    Rom. xiv. 10.
    2 Cor. v. 10.
    1 Pet. iv. 5.
    Rev. xx. 12.

Q. 4. What do they think concerning the union of Christ's Divinity with His Humanity?

A. Not like oil and water, but like wine and water they are joined together and are become One; and they believe in Him as Perfect God and Perfect Man both at His Conception and Birth, His Sufferings, Death, and Resurrection, and at His Coming at the last day; and that He had not destroyed (did not destroy) His Humanity by His Divinity, nor His Divinity by His Humanity.

Matt. i. 23.	Col. ii. 9.
John i. 14.	1 Cor. xv. 47.
John viii. 58.	1 John v. 20.

Q. 5. How do they believe in the Holy Ghost?

A. They believe that He proceeds from the Father, and that He is equal to both the Father and Son.

John i. 32.	Matt. iii. 16.
John xiv. 16, 26.	Mark i. 10.
John xv. 26.	

Q. 6. How many different Creeds have the Syrians?

A. They have only one Creed, called the Nicene Creed. It is as follows:—

THE CREED.

"I. We believe in the Almighty Father, the true and Only God; and we believe He is the Creator of Heaven and Earth, and of all things both visible and invisible:

"And in Jesus Christ, the Only Lord, Who is the Only Son of God; and we believe that He was begotten of the Father before all worlds; Light of Light; Very God of Very God; Begotten, not a Creature; Equal in essence to the Father; By Whose hand everything was made; and that He for us men, and for our salvation, descended from heaven, according to His Sovereign Will, and became Man, having taken His body from the Holy Ghost, and from the Virgin Mary who brought forth the God: He was crucified for us in the days of Pontius Pilate; He suffered, and was dead and buried; and that He rose on the third day, and ascended into Heaven, and sat on the right hand of His Father: and He, to Whose kingdom there is no end, cometh in great glory to judge both the dead and the quick.

"II. And in One Holy Ghost, Who quickens all, and Who is the Lord: and we believe that He proceeds from the Father, and is worshipped and glorified together with the Father and the Son, and that it was He that spake by the Prophets and Apostles.

" III. And in the One holy Church ; and we believe that it is the Catholic and the Apostolic Church ; and we acknowledge one Baptism for the remission of sins ; and we look for the Resurrection of the Dead, and for the New Life of the World to Come. Amen."

Q. 7. What is it that you say in this Creed, We believe in the One Holy Catholic Church ?

A. When the whole Church was going on in one only faith, certain men, differing as to the doctrine of the Holy Trinity, taught errors, and explained arguments mentioned in the Bible to suit this (their) erroneous opinions. Therefore, lest corruption should pervade the whole Church, the Fathers held meetings, and examined the whole Bible and its hidden mistiness (? mysteries), as well as the traditional doctrines of the Apostles[1]; and we believe the three holy Synods to be the Catholic Church, because those Synods established the doctrine of faith[2] in the Holy Trinity, and certain other rules, and put out all erroneous doctrines from the Church.

1. 2 Tim. ii. 2.   2 Thess. ii. 15.
   1 Cor. xi. 34.   2. Acts xx. 21.
   1 Cor. iv. 17.   Heb. vi. 12.
   Acts xviii. 11. Heb. xiii. 7.
   Phil. iv. 9.

Q. 8. Let me hear a brief account of those who taught errors, and of those three Synods which established the true faith.

A. First Arius the Bishop (*sic*) of Alexandria taught of the Humanity of Christ, that Christ was not the Creator, but a Creature; and that His body was not a real body, but that He feigned to be a man. Therefore, by the influence of Constantine the Great, a Synod of 318 Bishops was called together at Nice (Nicæa) A.D. 336[a], who, after having examined all the Scriptures, made the first part of the above Creed. And, as there were many[1] Gospels, they chose (the) four Gospels as four witnesses, and appointed the Canonical Books of the Old and New Testaments, and certain Fasts and Festivals, as also the Liturgy and the Canons, as well as a Patriarch in each of these places, Antioch, Rome, Constantinople, and Alexandria.

1. Rom. ii. 16.   Rom. xvi. 25.   2 Tim. ii. 8.

[a] In a very ancient Syrian Manuscript of Councils (14,528 in the British Museum) the Council of Nicæa is said to have been held "in the year 373 of the Computation of the Antiochians, and in the year 636 of the Computation of the Macedonians," i.e. A.D. 325. This MS. is of the early part of the sixth century.—ED.

Having thus divided the Earth into four parts, and given full power to each Patriarch in his Patriarchate, (and having) conducted the people orderly in one Faith, and (*rather*, they) deposed Arius, having pronounced a Curse[2] upon him.

2. 1 Cor. xvi. 22.	1 Cor. v. 5.
Gal. i. 8, 9.	2 John i. 10.
1 Thess. v. 14.	2 Thess. iii. 14.
1 Tim. i. 20.	

Furthermore, as is found in the Book containing Mar Ephraim's history, Mar Ephraim also went with Mar Jacob, Bishop of Nisibin, to this meeting; when all that was settled and sanctioned there was written by Mar Ephraim.

Secondly, Macedonious, the Patriarch of Constantinople, erred in the Doctrine of Faith in the Holy Ghost, (asserting) that He is not the Creator, but only a Creature; and that He proceeds not from the Father, but from the Son, as though He should obey the injunctions of the Son even in His Incarnation[b], and that He is a separate Being.

Therefore, by the instrumentality of Theodosius the Great, a meeting of one hundred and fifty Bishops was held at Constantinople, A.D. 394[c], when they drew up the second part of the above Creed, and sanctioned certain prayers and hymns made by Mar Ephraim and others to be inserted in the Service Book, and appointed certain Canons and Rules, and deposed Macedonious, having anathematized him, choosing in his room one Gregory Thevalogos.

Thirdly, Nestorious, the Patriarch of Constantinople, erroneously taught the Divinity of Christ; that the Virgin Mary brought forth only the Human Body of the Son of God, and not His Divinity; and (that) as He grew up, His Divinity was sometimes present with, and sometimes absent from, that Body; and that there are two distinct Natures, and two distinct Persons, and two distinct Wills in the Messiah; and that, therefore, the Virgin Mary should not be called *the Mother of God*, but only *the Mother of the Messiah* (or *Christ*), or *the Mother of the Son of Man.*

---

[b] This sentence is not clear.

[c] In the ancient MS. before alluded to, the date is thus given: "In the ninth year in the Consulship of Euchar and of Hevagrius, in the month Ab (August) of the year four hundred and twenty and nine of the Computation of the Antiochians." This is the same as A.D. 381, the date usually received.—ED.

Therefore, by the influence of Theodosius the younger, a Synod was called at Ephesus in A.D. 449 [d], consisting of 220 Bishops and Kalystinos (Celestinus or Cœlestinus) the Patriarch of Rome, Koorilos (Cyril) the Patriarch of Alexandria, and John, the Patriarch of Antioch, Chrisostom, who was also called Evanious (i.e. Evans or John) [e]; when they came to the same conclusion as that formerly held at Nice (Nicæa), namely, that Christ is perfect God and perfect Man, and that there is one Nature [f], one Person, and one Will in Christ; and

[d] The date usually received is A.D. 431; that of the *Latrocinium*, mentioned by our Author in the answer to Question 10, being usually assigned by the Western Church to the year 449.—ED.

[e] S. Chrysostom died A.D. 407, according to the accounts usually received among us.—ED.

[f] This important statement, bearing (as it does) on the very point at issue between the Jacobites and Catholics, ought surely to have been supported by a quotation from the language of the Council, or at least by a reference to the action or definition on which the author relies for his assertion. As it is, it is Cathanar Philipos's statement, and nothing more. Nevertheless, I have thought it my duty to examine the records of the Council of Ephesus with reference to this very point; and so much the more, because, as S. Cyril is known to have used the expression μιὰ φύσις σεσαρκωμένη with reference to our Lord after the Incarnation (Ep. i. ad Succensum), I thought it not improbable that some of his language, adopted by the Council, might peradventure seem to give some colour to our Author's statement. Of such expressions the following are the strongest that I have been able to discover:—

1. In his second Letter to Nestorius, S. Cyril wrote thus : " We affirm .... also that the Natures which were brought together unto true Oneness are indeed different ; yet of them both there is One Christ and Son : not as though the difference of the Natures were removed through the Union, but rather the Godhead and the Manhood, by their ineffable and inexpressible running together into Oneness, perfecting for us One Lord and Son, Jesus Christ."

Again, in the same Letter : "Thus will we confess One Christ and Lord, not as worshipping a Man together with the Word, that a fancy of a division may not be admitted by a side wind through saying *together with*—but as worshipping one and the same, because His Body is not foreign to the Word, nay He even sitteth therewith together with the Father Himself: not as though two Sons again are sitting together with (Him), but One, in regard of Union with His own Flesh. But if we decline to admit the Union in regard of Substance (Hypostatic Union), either as unintelligible or as unseemly, we fall into speaking of two Sons. For (there would be) all need to make a distinction, and to speak of the one, *properly* Man, as honoured by the appellation of the Son; but of the other again, *properly* the Word of God, as having naturally both name and reality of Sonship. We must not therefore divide into two that the Virgin Mary should be called *the Mother of God;* and (that) should any speak against these doctrines established and confirmed by the Synods of Nicæa, Constantinople, and Ephesus, he should be taken as a heretic, and excommunicated. And calling these three Synods the One and Only Catholic Church, they drew up the third part of the aforesaid Creed; and having cursed and deposed Nestorius, they appointed Maximus the Faster in his room.

Furthermore, in this meeting at Ephesus, Mar Chrysostom, who was also called Evanious, cried aloud first without fear, that the Virgin Mary was the Mother of God, when there came a voice from heaven, saying, "Thy mouth is of gold."

Sons, the One Lord Jesus Christ. But it will in no wise advance the right account of the Faith, that it should be so, even if some add as a saving clause a Union of Persons: for the Scripture hath not said that the Word united a man's Person to Himself, but that He was made Flesh."—*Labbe and Cossart*, iii. 869, 872, ed. Coleti.

2. In his third Letter S. Cyril, alluding to S. John's statement that "The Word was made Flesh, and dwelt among us," coupled with that of S. Paul, that "in Him dwelt all the fulness of the Godhead bodily," says that It dwelt in Him not as It is said to dwell in the saints; but that rather the Word, being united in respect of Nature, and not turned into flesh, made such an indwelling as the human soul may be said to have in regard to its proper body. "Christ, then," he adds, "is One, not as though Man held simply a conjunction with God, such as consists in oneness of dignity or authority with God: for equality in honour does not unite Natures. Nor do we understand the mode of the conjunction by way of apposition; for this is not sufficient for a natural Union (ἔνωσιν φυσικήν); nor yet by way of affectual (qy. relative or sympathetic) participation (μέθεξιν σχετικήν), in which respect we also are joined to the Lord, as it is written, &c., yea rather we do repudiate the name Conjunction (συναφεία), as insufficient to declare this Union."— *Labbe and Cossart*, iii. 949.

3. Lastly, in the Anathemas subjoined to this Letter we have the following: "If any one, in the One Christ, divide the Substances after the Union, connecting them only by a conjunction in respect of dignity, that is to say authority or power, and not rather by a concourse in respect of natural union: let him be accursed."

I will not trust myself to make any comment on the foregoing extracts: but will only add that the second Letter was accepted by the Council in Action I. by acclamation; and that the third with the Anathemas, was also apparently accepted by the Council—though the discussion went off into a question as to whether the Letter had been duly given to Nestorius—for the Council expressly acknowledge S. Cyril's Letters (in the plural) as agreeable to the Nicene Creed in all respects. See the Council's Letter to the Emperors. [*Labbe and Cossart*, iii. 1100.]—ED.

Therefore he is to this day called Chrysostom, interpreted the Gold-mouthed.

Q. 9. Can you mention what the different passages are, which were falsely explained by Arious and the rest, to suit their opinion in matters of faith?

A. 1. That of Arious:—

Matt. xvii. 2.   Mark xiii. 32.   Luke iv. 30.
          John x. 29; (and) xiv. 2S.

2. That of Macedonious:—

John xvi. 7, 14; (and) xx. 22.

3. That of Nestorius:—

Matt. xix. 17; and xxvi. 39.   Luke xxii. 44.
Mark xv. 34.   John xi. 34.

Q. 10. Were there no other Synods of the Fathers besides these?

A. There was a second Synod convened at Ephesus, besides several others assembled on different occasions, but none of which (them) is considered as a holy Synod. The name Holy Catholic Church, properly belongs to the above-mentioned *three* Synods collectively.

Eutychus, a priest of Constantinople, asserted that God the Messiah was compelled to suffer and die against His Will, and he was therefore excommunicated by Ablanious (Flavianus) the Patriarch of Constantinople, but on his repentance, it became a question whether he could be received back into the Church. To settle the question, a second Synod was convened at Ephesus in the year 451, consisting of 130 Bishops. The Patriarch(s) of Antioch and Rome did not join it. The Synod considered the questions (question) whether Eutychus could be admitted to the Church without re-baptism. It was inferred from the Creed that there is only one Baptism for the remission of sins, and Eutychus was on that ground received without a re-baptism.

Q. 11. Upon what grounds in Scripture did Eutychus make the abovesaid heretical assertions?

A. Matt. xxvi. 39; Mark xiv. 34, 36; Luke xxii. 42—44.

Q. 12. Do those above-mentioned four Patriarchs still continue their former friendship and unanimity of purpose?

A. With the exception of the Pope, who is the Patriarch of Rome, the other three continue to hold the same doctrines.

Q. 13. What is the cause of the Pope's separation?

A. Pope Leo adopted certain of the heresies of Arius and
the rest, and made a mixture of the true faith with false doctrines, (asserting):—

1. That the two Natures of Christ, namely, His Divinity
and His Humanity, are like oil and water; and that He is
One Person; and that His Divinity had gone from Him at
the time of His Death.

2. That the Holy Ghost proceeds from both the Father
and the Son.

Having thus (therefore) drawn up his faith, and a certain
Liturgy, he, by the favour of Bulkara (Pulcheria), the Queen
of Rome, and her husband Markanos (Marcianus), whom he
had gained over to his interest, called together a Synod in
A.D. 472 [g], at Chalcedon, consisting of 636 Bishops, Priests,
and Deacons. With a view to make this meeting more re-
markable, and its Canons more stable than the Nicene Insti-
tutions, determined by 318 Fathers, he forced these 636 persons to sign the Institutes against their will; threatening
those who would not conform to this Council with severe
punishments. Thus he propagated these doctrines in all those
countries then included in the Roman Empire; and on the
Pope sending the large book containing the new Rules and
Offices for the members of this Synod to read and affire
(affix) their signatures, Deuscorous, the Patriarch of Alexandria, took and read it, and then sent it back, having written
in it, "He who conforms to this (these) rules is cursed," and
afflired (affixed) his signature to it. This caused a great
quarrel, and the Pope having taken Deuscorous and his partisans, confined them on the sea-shore, where they died. It
is on account of this that the Papists curse Deuscorous and
his partisans, at the time of their Ordination. And the Pope,
it is said, altered certain words in the Bible, in order that
those errors which he supported in the Synod should be justi-
fied. Besides this, he made some alterations in the Creed,
too. For there is some difference between the Creeds of the
Italians, Maronites, and Chaldeans, who are all Papists.

Q. 14. You say that the Synod of Chalcedon established
a Faith partly true and partly false. Explain how it was.

A. (1.) The Synod of Nice (Nicæa) established the true
faith, that the Son of God was of *One* Nature and of *One* Per-

---

[g] The date usually received is A.D. 451; Marcian died in 457.

son. Nestoreos said that He was of *Two* Natures and of Two Persons. The Synod of Chalcidon (*sic*) proposed that he was of *Two* Natures and of *One* Person: that Christ died in the Nature of Man, and that His Second Coming is also in the Nature of Man.

(2.) The Synod of Nice (Nicæa)[h] called Mary *the Mother of God*; Nestorious called her *the Mother of Man*; the Chalcidon Synod called her *Virgin Mary*.

(3.) The Nicen (Nicene) Synod proposed that the Birth, Death, &c., of Christ was *of His own accord*; Eutichos said that Christ died *against His Will*; (the) Chalcidonian Synod said that Christ died *to fulfil the Prophecy*.

(4.) Nice (Nicæa)[i]—The Holy Ghost proceedeth *from the Father*; Maccedonious (Macedonius)—the Holy Ghost proceedeth *from the Son*; Calceedon (sic)—the Holy Ghost proceedeth *from the Father and Son*.

Q. 15. Can it be shewn that such discrepancies exist in the Creed?

[h] Rather Ephesus, in adopting the Anathemas of S. Cyril. And Chalcedon in the Definition of the Faith.—ED.

[i] The Nicene Creed, according to very ancient copies of it, including the Syriac copy already mentioned—and I suppose no older MS. of the Councils is known, at least in Europe—ran thus : " And I believe in the Holy Ghost." The Council of Constantinople added the words " Who proceedeth from the Father." The words *and the Son* were added, it is thought, first at the third Council of Toledo, A.D. 589, at the instigation of King Reccared. See the Council, in Labbe (ed. Coleti), vi. 697. Mr. Ffoulkes gives an able *resumé* of this matter, and of the subsequent history of the *Filioque* clause, in " The Church's Creed, or the Crown's Creed ?"

But although the clause was, so far as is known, now first added to the Niceno-Constantinopolitan Creed, we certainly hear of it before. I do not propose to enter into the question at any length, and will merely add the following memorandum :—

The *Filioque*, or *And the Son*, clause.

We find it A.D. 400.   Toledo I., in a Creed altogether different from that of Nicæa. Labbe, vol. ii. p. 1475.

A.D. 411.   Braga I., IF genuine. Labbe, iii. 345.

A.D. 431.   In S. Cyril to Nestorius. Labbe, iii. 956.
            Pagi says that S. Cyril was taken to task for it : see extract in Labbe, iii. 347. But the Letter was adopted by the Council of Ephesus.

A.D. 589.   Toledo III., as stated above.

Cf. also the Letter of Hormisdas to the Eastern Emperor.—ED.

C

A. It will be seen from the following statement:—

SYRIANS.	MARONIT(E)S THE PAPISTS.	PAPISTS (sic.)	PAPISTS (sic.)
Nicene Creed.	Nicene Creed.	Creed.	Apostles' Creed.
We believe	We believe	I believe	I believe
From the [1] Virgin Mother of God	Of the Virgin Mary	Of the Virgin Mary	Of the Virgin Mary
Dead [2]	Dead	o	Dead
As His will [3]	According to the Scriptures	According to the Scriptures	o
He cometh [4]	He cometh	He shall come	He shall come
He sat [5]	He sat	He sitteth	He sitteth
Proceedeth from the Father [6]	Proceedeth from the Father and the Son.	Proceedeth from the Father and the Son	o
In One Church, the Catholic and Apostolic	In One Church, the Catholic and Apostolic	One Catholic and Apostolic Romish Church	In the Holy Catholic Church
In One God the Father	In One God the Father	In One God the Father	In God the Father
In One Lord Jesus	In One Lord Jesus	In One Lord Jesus	In Jesus
In One Holy Ghost	In One Holy Ghost	In the Holy Ghost	In the Holy Ghost

1. Luke i. 43.   Rom. viii. 34.   4. Jude i. 14.
   Luke ii. 11.   3. John x. 18.   5. Mark xvi. 19.
   John xx. 28.   Gal. i. 4.   6. John xiv. 16.
2. Heb. ii. 9.   Titus ii. 14.   John xv. 26.

Q. 16. What is the belief of the Syrians with reference to the duration of the fulness of Godhead and Manhood of Christ; viz. its end?

A. The Syrians believe that Christ was (*sie*) fully God and fully Man until the time shewn 1 Cor. xv. 28, where it is said, " Then shall the Son also Himself be subject unto Him that put all things under Him, that God may be all in all." God in the first place created Man with earth [1], and second (secondly) endowed (him) with a spirit. But the name Adam his allusion (? alludes) only to the first occurrence, and not to the second. Again Christ converted Water into Wine at Galilee ; hence it is said that they drank water [2] in allusion to the predicate water. In the same way, God first descended into the belly (womb) of the Virgin, and then took flesh. And in reference to the first occurrence, viz. the Descent of God, the Syrians believe

1. 1 Moses ii. 7 ; v. 2.   2. John ii. 9.

that *God* was born, that *God* died, and that the Virgin Mary is the Mother of God.

Q. 17. Why are the Syrians called Jacobites?

A. When Nestorious and his partisans insisted on many Bishops and people conforming to and using the newly-made doctrine, and threatened those who refused compliance, the Saint Mar Jacob Boordana (Baradæus), who was clothed with skin[1], coming to know of this from God, when he was living in the woods[2], how the Nestorians had subverted and hindered the true faith, came out from his seclusion and boldly exhorted many, and turned them to the true faith. Therefore they are called Jacobites, by which we understand those who were redeemed from the Nestorians by the means of Mar Jacob.

1. Heb. xi. 37.　　　　　　　　2. Heb. xi. 38.

Q. 18. What is their belief concerning the holy Ceremony of the Kooroobana and the Bread and Wine?

A. They believe the Offering of the Kooroobana to be a holy Sacrifice[1], and the Bread and Wine in it to be the real Body and Blood of Christ[2].

1. 1 Pet. ii. 5.	1 Cor. x. 16.
Heb. xiii. 15.	1 Cor. xi. 27.
2. Matt. xxvi. 26.	John vi. 53, 55.
Matt. xxvii. 28.	

Argument.—As it is said in the fourth verse of the first chapter of St. John's Gospel that the Word was made Flesh; and as God, Who is the Word, became Flesh and Blood; so by Word, these also, i.e. Bread and Wine, become Flesh and Blood.

Q. 19. As (Does) the Syrian Church allow the partaking of the Consecrated Wine, just as they do of the Consecrated Bread?

A. In the time of Consecration the Bread and Wine are mixed, and as (the) Bread is a mixture of Wine (probably = is mixed with the Wine), therefore the mixed Bread is usually given. Acts xx. 7, ii. 42.

Q. 20. How do they honour and regard the Mother of God and all the Saints?

A. They do them honour[1] and worship as due to them, thinking they are holy persons and the friends of God[2]. But they do not hold them in the same light as they do God, or give them (the) praise and worship which are due to God alone.

1. Rom. xiii. 7.	James ii. 23.
Luke i. 48.	2 Chron. xx. 7.
James v. 11.	Isaiah xli. 8.
2. John xi. 11.	

Q. 21. Do they remember Saints in their Churches?

A. They remember and celebrate the birthdays and days of death of some of the Saints, but only the days of death of some Saints (others).

Matt. xxvi. 13.	Ps. cxii. 6.
2 Moses xxviii. 12.	Prov. x. 7.

Q. 22. Do they pray to the Saints?

A. They pray to the Saints to pray to God on their behalf, and they not only think that the Saints will hear their prayers, and pray for them to God, but they also expect that God will help them for the sake of the Saints.

Luke xvi. 27, 28.	1 Sam. xxviii. 14, 19.
Acts xix. 12.	1 Kings xi. 12.
Rom. i. 9.	2 Kings xiii. 21.
Eph. i. 16.	2 Kings xix. 34.
Heb. xii. 23.	2 Kings xx. 6.
Rev. viii. 4.	Tobit xii. 12.
Rev. v. 8.	2 Mac. xv. 12.

Q. 23. Do they pray for the Dead?

A. They pray for the Dead.

1 Cor. xv. 29.	Nehem. ix. 2.
Eph. vi. 18.	2 Mac. xii. 34, 45.

Q. 24. Do they observe fasting, either entire or partial, and do they expect any good from it?

A. During some fast days they entirely abstain from food; and during others they eat very little, and administer all their holy rites with fasting. Besides this they fast on Wednesdays and Fridays, and believe that much good is derived from fasting.

Matt. iv. 2.	Judges xiii. 4.
Matt. xvii. 21.	Esther iv. 16.
Luke xviii. 12.	Jonah iii. 5.
Acts xiii. 3.	Joel i. 14.
2 Moses xxxiv. 28.	Nehem. ix. 1.
4 Moses vi. 3.	

Q. 25. Do they found Churches in the name of Saints?

A. There is not one Syrian Church which is not named

either by the Name of the Mother of God or of one of the Saints.

| 1 Kings xviii. 31. | Eph. ii. 20. | Rev. xxi. 14. |

Q. 26. Do they confess their sins before the Priests?

A. It is commanded that all persons above seven years of age should confess their sins.

Matt. iii. 6.	1 John i. 9.
Acts xix. 18.	Nehem. ix. 2.
James v. 16.	Prov. xxviii. 13.

Q. 27. Do they make holy oil, and anoint men with it?

A. Three ointments are ordained : two to anoint those who are baptized, and one to anoint the sick. Holy Mooron, the chief of these, is consecrated by the Patriarch. Metrans have power to consecrate the other two.

1 Moses xxviii. 18.	James v. 14.
2 Moses xxx. 30.	1 John ii. 20, 27.
Mark vi. 13.	

Q. 28. Do they make the form (sign) of the Cross with their fingers, by touching with them first their forehead, then the breast, and then the two shoulders: and (do they) worship the Cross and place it in their churches?

A. In all holy actions they make the form of the Cross[1] with their fingers, by touching with them their forehead, breast, and shoulders; and (they) worship[k] it[2], and place it in their churches.

1. Gal. vi. 14.	1 Moses xxxiii. 3.
1 Cor. i. 18.	1 Moses xlii. 6.
Phil. iii. 18.	1 Moses xlviii. 12.
Matt. xxiv. 30.	2 Moses xviii. 7.
2. Ps. xcix. 5, 9.	

Q. 29. Do they prohibit the Clergy from getting married?

A. It is appointed that a layman or a Deacon who has once got married, and whose wife is still alive, may become a Priest; and when an unmarried Deacon is once ordained a Priest he may not get married; and one who has married a widow, or bondwoman, or any of low extraction, should not be ordained a Priest.

| 1 Tim. iii. 2, 11. | Titus i. 6. |

---

[k] I believe this signifies nothing more than regard it with veneration.—ED.

Q. 30. Have they any objection to give the Order of Priests to one who is unmarried ?

A. They have no objection. And they have appointed to give the Order of Priests to one who likes to live in convents, notwithstanding his unmarried state. 1 Cor. vii. 7, viii. 32. But if one who was ordained a Priest after his marriage get married a second time, after the death of his first wife, and one who was consecrated to the office of Priest when the vow of celibacy was upon him, gets married, these two are regarded as having fallen from their office.

Q. 31. Do they consecrate married men to the office of Patriarch and Bishop ?

A. They consecrate those who keep the vow of celibacy, and those who keep that vow on the death of their first wives, to the office of Bishops, but only those who keep the vow of perpetual celibacy to the office of Patriarchs.

1 Cor. vii. 1.   Rev. xiv. 4.

Q. 32. How many kinds of holy Orders are there ?

A. The following three : 1st, Bishops ; 2nd, Priests ; 3rd, Deacons.

Q. 33. What are the different degrees in the office of Bishops ?

A. The following three : 1st, Patriarch ; 2nd, Mapriana [i.e. Catholic] ; 3rd, Metropolitan, or Episcop.

Q. 34. What is the authority invested in the office of a Patriarch ?

A. He is the overruler and lord of everything connected with the Syrian Church.

Q. 35. What is the authority invested in the office of a Mapriana ?

A. He can do everything belonging to the office of a Patriarch, with his sanction. He is the heir, if he likes, to the office of Patriarch, on the death of the then living Patriarch, and he signs himself the Chief Bishop of the Eastern Countries, or the Chief Bishop of the Tigris.

Q. 36. What is the authority of a Metropolitan ?

A. He is to govern the different Parishes entrusted to his care by the Patriarch, and to ordain both Priests and Deacons.

Q. 37. How many kinds of Priests are there ?

A. The following three :—1st, Rampan ; 2ndly, Chor-Episcopa ; 3rdly, Kashisha.

Q. 38. What is the difference between these three kinds of Priests?

A. 1st, Rampan is one who lives in convents, having taken upon him the vow of celibacy. Chor-Episcopa is one who has married, and whose business it is to report to the Metropolitan after having investigated serious matters in the Church, to examine the Priests, and to appoint whatever is deficient in the Church government and reprove those who are in error. 3rdly, Kashisha is one who has married, and is a ruler in his own parish.

Q. 39. How many kinds of Deacons are there?

A. The following three:—1st, Archdeacon; 2ndly, Mashamshana; 3rdly, Hypodiaconon (Sub-deacon).

Q. 40. What is the difference between these three orders of Deacons?

A. 1st, Archdeacon is the chief Deacon, whose business it is to examine the Deacons, and to help the Bishops when Ordination, and such holy services, take place; 2ndly, Meshamshana; 3rdly, Hypodiaconon. These are to help the Priests in all the holy services of the Church, and they have authority to read both the Old (Testament) and the Epistles in the Churches. But they have no authority to read the Gospel in the Churches.

Q. 41. Who are the Karoya and the Masamarana?

A. They are children who have received permission from the Metran to sing Psalms in the Churches.

Q. 42. Can a Metran consecrate a man to the office of Metran, with the sanction of the Patriarch, as is the custom of the Papists?

A. If it is the Patriarch himself that consecrates a Metran, he must do it in conjunction with two or three other Metrans. Besides this, even the Patriarch has no power to permit a Metran to consecrate another as a Metran. But on just and reasonable grounds it is appointed that three Metrans should come together and consecrate a Metran, with the sanction of the Patriarch.

Matt. xviii. 20.   Acts xiii. 3.

Q. 43. Do they confer special names on the Bishops besides their own names?

A. The person who was appointed to the office of Bishop at Antioch, after the death of St. Peter, was St. Ignatheous

(Ignatius), the child whom our Lord took in His arms[1], and who afterwards became the disciple of St. John the Evangelist. Therefore all the Patriarchs of Antioch are called Ignatheous after his name. Those who are appointed to the office of Maphriana are called Baselious (Basil). Those who are consecrated to the office of Bishop of Jerusalem are called Gregorious. And all the other Bishops are called by any one of the following twelve names, as the Patriarch chooses :—

Severious (Severus).	Julios (Julius).
Theoscorus (Dioscorus).	Pelexcinos (Philloxenus).
Athanasious (Athanasius).	Authemos.
Dewanasious (Dionysius).	Clemis (Clement)
Timotheos (Timothy).	Coorilos (Cyril).
Osthatheos (Eustathius).	Ewanious (Evans).

1. Matt. xviii. 2.   Mark ix. 36.

Q. 44. When are these offices and names conferred upon them ?

A. All the Dignities belonging to Holy Orders are given to them during the Koorbana. Then this name also is given by the person by whom (the) consecration is performed.

Q. 45. Has the Bishop of Jerusalem more authority and dignity than the rest of the Bishops ?

A. He has no special dignity in his office and authority. Yet because he is the Metropolitan of the Holy City, he is considered as a general[1] and eminent Bishop, and [m] calls him the Fifth Patriarch.

Q. 46. How are the Syrian Priests [Catanars] supported ?

A. They are supported by portions from Laity allowed them for certain religious ceremonies.

Q. 47. Do the Syrians think that those who do not conform to the persuasion of the Patriarch of Antioch will not be saved, as the Papists say ?

A. They do not think as the Papists do, but believe that God through His mercy[1] will give eternal salvation to those who (are) baptized, and who believe in the Trinity in the proper way, and keep the commandments contained in the

1. Luke xiii. 24.   John vi. 44, 65.
   Eph. ii. 8.   Rom. ix. 15, 16.

[1] May this be a translation of *Catholicos ?* See Q. 33.—ED.
[m] Some word omitted. Cf. Canon 7 of Nicæa.—ED.

37th, 38th, (and) 39th verses of the twenty-second chapter of St. Matthew.

Q. 48. Do they believe in the existence of Purgatory?

A. They do not believe in the existence of such a place.

Q. 49. Do they make images and worship them?

A. No.

Q. 50. In what light do they hold the Pope now?

A. In the same light the Protestants hold him.

Q. 51. What are the hours of prayer in the Church?

A. Every morning and evening all the priests assemble in the Church¹, when they pray and read portions of the Bible, as regulated in their office-book, and offer Incense². But on certain Festivals, and during Lent, and on other Fast-days, they pray³ thrice a-day, and perform the other Rites as explained above.

1. Acts iii. 1.	3. Ps. lv. 17.
2. 2 Moses xxx. 7.	Dan. vi. 10.
Luke i. 11.	

Q. 52. In the answer of the 24th question you told me that they observed certain Fast-days. How many Fast-days are there in a year?

A. Seven.

Q. 53. Let me hear an account of these.

A. 1. Fast-days of Nineveh; they begin on Monday and end on Thursday. 2. Bawoosa Fast-day ⁿ; it ends on the seventh day. 3. Lent; it ends on the 50th day, the day of our Lord's Resurrection. These are changeable Fast-days. 4. Fast-days of our Lord's Nativity, which commence on December 1st, and end on the 25th of the same month, the day of our Lord's Birth. 5. The Fast-days of the Apostles, beginning on the 16th of June, and ending on the 29th, the Festival day of the Apostles Peter and Paul. 6. The Fast-days of the Virgin, which commence on the 1st of August, and end on the 15th, the holy day which is the Ascension-day of the Virgin Mary. 7. The Fasting of the Virgin. It commences on the 1st of September, and ends on the 8th, the holy day of the Birth of the Virgin Mary.

Q. 54. How do they know when to observe the Festival of Easter?

A. The date (rather, the method) of calculating the Day

ⁿ I should have spelled it Baootho or Boütho. The Malabar Syrians pronounce the Syriac letter *tau* as *s.*—ED.

of (the) Resurrection depends upon an epoch made by Ebese-
vios, and upon the numbers of the days of the year and
month ; and it is from these that the Day of (the) Resurrection, and all other moveable Feasts and Fasts, are determined.
Although it is difficult to make a translation of its computation, but (yet) I will try to make a translation. I will en-
deavour to give an example of it. That (this) is a Table of
the moveable Fasts for the next ten years according to the
above calculation :—

A Table of some of the Moveable Fasts, Syrian Date.

Year.	Fast of Nineveh.	Lent.	Easter Sunday.
1867	February 6	February 26	April 16
1868	January 21	February 10	March 31
1869	February 10	March 2	April 20
1870	February 2	February 22	April 12
1871	January 18	February 7	March 28
1872	February 6	February 26	April 16
1873	January 29	February 18	April 8
1874	January 21	February 10	March 31
1875	February 3	February 23	April 13
1876	January 25	February 14	April 4

Q. 55. When is the New Year of the Syrians ?

A. The 1st of January is their New Year('s Day). This
1st of January of the Syrians is the 13th of January with
the Europeans. This difference, therefore, exists in all the
months.

The Days of Every Month :—

January (Second Chanon)	.	31	July (Thamuz)	31
February (Shebat)	. . .	28	August (Ab)	31
March (Adar)	..	31	September (Elul)	30
April (Nisan)		30	October (First Teshrin) . .	31
May (Iyar)		31	November (Second Teshrin)	30
June (Chaziran)		30	December (First Chanon) .	31

Q. 56. On what special days, and at what time, is the Holy
Koorobana administered?

A. It is administered chiefly on Sundays and Holidays,
and other days as occasions require, before 12 o'clock in the
day, with fasting.

Acts ii. 42; xx. 7.

Q. 57. Have the Bishops and Priests any dress of honour
indicating their office ?

A. They have dresses of honour.

2 Moses xxxix. 1, 27, 41.   1 Sam. xxii. 18.

Q. 58. What is the belief of the Syrians with regard to the saying of some who assert that Joseph knew the Virgin Mary after the birth of the Lord, and that she brought him forth children; since it is said in the 25th verse of the 2nd (1st) chapter of St. Matthew, "He knew her not till she had brought forth her first-born son?"

A. They believe that she never afterwards brought forth children, but that she is a holy, and perfect, and perpetual Virgin; just as we cannot think that Michal, the daughter of Saul, brought forth children after her death, since it is said in the 23rd verse of the 6th chapter of the 2nd Book of Samuel, "Therefore Michal, the daughter of Saul, had no child unto the day of her death º."

Q. 59. Who do they think was the Mother of James, Joses, &c., who are spoken of as the Brethren of our Lord, in the 55th verse of the 13th chapter of St. Matthew's Gospel?

A. They think them to be the sons of (another) Mary (that) she brought forth to Joseph ᵖ, she being supposed to be the married wife of Joseph (*sic*), and one of the women who ministered to our Lord.

Matt. xxvii. 56.   Mark xv. 40, 47.   John xix. 25.

Q. 60. Where do the Souls of the Saints stay till the Judgment Day?

A. It is supposed that they stay in Paradise.

Luke xxiii. 43.

Inference. They believe that the Souls of the Saints abide in Paradise till the Judgment Day, since the Paradise from which Adam was expelled is to be enjoyed by Adam and his descendants, and since it is said in the 3rd verse of the 14th chapter of St. John's Gospel, "I will come again and receive you unto Myself."

Q. 61. Which (of what kind) is the abode of the Souls of the Wicked till the Day of Judgment?

A. They live in utter sorrow, in a place of fire and darkness.

2 Pet. ii. 4, 9.   Jude i. 7.

º One might add Gen. xxviii. 15; Ps. cxii. 8; Dan. i. 21, &c.—ED.

ᵖ This must surely be a clerical error for Alphæus or Cleophas. Cf. Matt. x. 3; Mark xv. 40; John xix. 25.—ED.

Q. 62. When are they put in possession of Heaven and Hell?

A. It is supposed that it is after their Judgment.

Matt. xxv. 46.   John v. 29.   Rom. ii. 5, 6.

Q. 63. Do the Saints also judge Sinners?

A. Yes, they do judge the Sinners.

Matt. xix. 28.   Rev. iii. 21; and xx. 4.
Luke xxii. 30.   Dan. vii. 22.
1 Cor. vi. 2.

Q. 64 q. What Books do ʼthey (the Syrians) receive (as) Canonical?

A. The following Books:—

THE OLD TESTAMENT.

1 Moses.	Job.	Habakkuk.
2 Moses.	Psalms.	Zephaniah.
3 Moses.	Proverbs.	Haggai.
4 Moses.	Ecclesiastes.	Zechariah.
5 Moses.	Song of Solomon.	Malachi.
Joshua.	Isaiah.	Rest of Esther.
Judges.	Jeremiah.	Rest of Ezra.
Ruth.	Lamentations.	Tobias.
1 Samuel.	Ezekiel.	Judith.
2 Samuel.	Daniel.	Wisdom.
1 Kings.	Hosea.	Jesus,the Son of Sirach.
2 Kings.	Joel.	Baruch.
1 Chronicles.	Amos.	Song of the 3 Children.
2 Chronicles.	Obadiah.	Susannah.
Ezra.	Jonah.	Bel and the Dragon.
Nehemiah.	Micah.	Manasses.
Esther.	Nahum.	Maccabees.

THE NEW TESTAMENT.

The Four Gospels.   Revelation.
The Acts.   The Canons and Liturgy as re-
Twenty-one Epistles.   gulated by the Fathers ʳ.

q Between *Q.* 63 and 64, the following was inserted and afterwards crossed out: " *Q.* 64. Are the Heaven and the Hell everlasting? or is there any end to their existence? *A.* The Treatise my Father, Rev. Philipos made in Malayalim on."—Ed.

ʳ One would be glad to know the source whence this list is derived. It looks as if it were compiled from a combination of the Canonical and Apocryphal Books mentioned in the Sixth Article of the Church of England, with the addition of "The Canons and Liturgy." It may be

Q. 65. Are there any other books besides these written by the Fathers of the old times, and the Fathers of later times?

A. Those written by the Fathers of the old times are the Book of Asenath, the wife of Joseph : the History of the destruction of Jerusalem, by Titus ; the History of King Herod; the Book of Josephus, &c. There are many Books written by the Fathers of later times, viz. Mar Ephraim, Mar Jacob, Clement, Severus, Gregorius, &c. These Books have become scarce now, since they are manuscripts to this day, and some are not even extant now.

Q. 66. How many Patriarchs are said to have occupied the Chair of St. Peter at Antioch?

A. Including the present Patriarch there have been 142 Patriarchs. Some of them were martyrs, being persecuted and killed by the Jews, Romans, Nestorians, and Mahomedans. Some were oppressed and persecuted. So most of them lived a life of great sorrow and misery. Moreover, it is to be found in some books of the Fathers that the persecutions of the Mahomedans were not so severe as those of the Romans.

Q. 67. What is the name of the present Patriarch of Antioch?

A. His name is Jacob the second, Mar Egnatheous (Ignatius). His Holiness lives in the Convent called in the Syriac Koorkuma, and in the Arabic, Sapran, which is in the town of Marden ⁸ in Turkey.

Q. 68. Is there any one besides who is called the Patriarch of Antioch?

A. In (A.D.) 1427, Maron, the Bishop of the Churches on the mountains of Lebanon, rebelled against the Patriarch of Antioch, and joined the Pope, together with the Churches under his care. He displaced the Prayers of the Liturgy,

observed that (apart from the addition last spoken of) the list is not exactly that of the Vulgate, nor of the ancient Syriac Version of the Holy Scriptures called the Peschito, nor of the Council of Laodicea—indeed no Syriac MS. of that Council that I have seen, and I have examined several, contains a nominal list of the Sacred Books (Mr. B. H. Cowper, with a much larger experience of the Syriac MSS., bore the same testimony in personal conversation with myself)—nor, lastly, is it that of the list of the Apostolical Canons, as it is found in either Syriac or Greek copies.—ED. P.S. I am not sure about the Peschito list.

⁸ Lat. 37° 15′, Lon. 40° 40′.—ED.

making the first last, and the last first [t], besides adopting the belief of the Pope. He calls himself Patriarch of Antioch, but no one would (will) acknowledge him as the Patriarch of Antioch. His followers are chiefly called Maronites. There are two or three Bishops besides, who, being excommunicated by the Patriarch on account of their misconduct, joined the Pope, and embraced his religion. Their followers have increased in number, and they rule the churches in Bagdad, and in the neighbouring places, and the Pope has conferred on one of them the title of the Patriarch of Antioch. Even this creature of a Patriarch is ashamed to sign himself as the Patriarch. Their followers have not yet been called by any general name.

Q. 69. By whom was the Church of the Syrians in Malabar founded and governed?

A. In A.D. 52. The Apostle Mar Thomas came to Malabar in the reign of Choshen. He was so successful in his preaching that seven Christian churches were founded by him there [u]. But for a long time after his death Christianity was in a declining state in Malabar. But as India and the countries in the East fell to the share of the Patriarch of Antioch in the Nicene Synod, he appointed a Maphriana at Tigris in Bagdad, to conduct all the religious affairs of the Eastern Churches under the care of the Patriarch. This Maphriana, coming to know from Thoma, a prince of Canan, of the decline of the Churches in Malabar, informed the Patriarch of the same; when, in pursuance to (of) the orders of the Patriarch, he sent the above-mentioned prince Thoma, and Joseph the Bishop, a native of Orfa [x], and other Bishops, Priests, and Deacons, and a Colony of Syrians with their families. They

---

[t] This perhaps alludes to the Invocation of the Holy Ghost in the Liturgy. See Dr. Neale's Malabar Lit., or Renaudot, or my " Christians of S. Thomas," p. 40, for an example of a similar transposition.—ED.

[u] That there was communication between Rome and the Malabar coast in the Apostles' days is beyond a doubt. Roman coins of this period are frequently found in the neighbourhood. In May, 1812, an earthen pot was found near Coimbatore, containing 522 silver denarii, 135 of which were coins of Augustus, 378 more of Tiberius. See the account of these and others in the Madras Journal of Literature and Science, for 1844-5, vol. xiv. p. 212. The editor has in his possession an Aureus of the Emperor Tiberius, which, with "several hundred" more, none later than Nero, were found near Calicut, about 1850.

[x] i.e. Uraha or Edessa, as appears from a letter in the Editor's possession.

landed at Kodungaloor [y] in the reign of Cheruan (Cheruman) Perumal [z], A.D. 345, when the king received them gladly, and gave them certain privileges and names of honour as accounted by the natives, and a place to live in. By them and their successors to the office of Bishop who came from Antioch, were the Syrian Churches founded (? = firmly settled) and governed.

When the Syrian Church was in this state, the Portuguese not only persecuted and killed all the Bishops as they came from Antioch, but their Metran, Dom Pre Alleskes De Menesis (Alexius de Menezes), residing at Goa, came to the Malayalim country in 1598, and having visited all the Syrian Churches, (he) bribed the petty princes then ruling the country, and some Syrians, in order to gain them over to his interest. And those Syrians who opposed his designs were persecuted and put to death. So by main force he assembled all the Syrians in the Church at Odyamperoor and persuaded them to embrace Popery, besides burning all the Syriac Bibles, and many other Syriac books. Then all the married priests were separated from their wives. (Menezes) also drew up a book regulating their future mode of living, and enjoined a strict obedience to these laws on the part of the Syrians. And any one may know the great enmity and wickedness which this Alleskes practised towards the Syrian Church, if he thoughtfully reads that book containing his visit news (? visit-news) of the different churches, printed in Portuguese, in 1606, in the office of Deogoo Gomis Low Tire, printer, of

[y] This place, anciently called Mahodeverpatnam, and more recently Cranganore, lies at the mouth of a small river in lat. 10°, 13'.—ED.

[z] The dynasty of the Perumals is thought by a writer in the Royal Asiatic Soc. Jour., vii. 343, to have flourished in the ninth century. Whatever may have been their date, there are still extant in Malabar two very ancient documents, inscribed on copper plates, facsimiles of which, with translations, may be seen in the Madras Journal of Literature and Science, vol. xiii. part 1, (and facsimiles alone in the Royal Asiatic Society's Journal, vol. vii.). One of these documents consists of a single plate inscribed on both sides, and is a grant from the Rajah Vira Raghava Chacravarti (apparently one of the Perumals) to one Iravi Corttan of Mahodeverpatnam, creating him Grand Merchant of the Cheraman world, and conferring on him certain privileges of nobility, with the Lordship of the Manigramam (which word appears to signify a Christian, or perhaps a Manichean, community). The other, a much longer document, is a grant of land and privileges to the Tarisa Church built by Isodata Virai. The plates are in the college at Cottayam.—ED.

a place called Vni Wersi Dadi, in the country Coempra in Goa. After this, in 1685, Mar Evanious the Bishop came from Antioch, and with much difficulty redeemed the now existing Syrian churches from the Portuguese; and those Churches which could not be reclaimed by Mar Evanious still continue Romish: yet their Liturgy is to this day in the Syriac.

Q. 70. Did any of the Syrians in Malabar rise against the Portuguese before this Mar Evanious came from Antioch?

A. A priest named Itly Thomen, of the Church at Kallus-herry, in Malabar, boldly came forward and fought well with the Portuguese. He made certain rules for strengthening the Syrian Churches, and wrote certain books for the same. The Portuguese often sought diligently to kill him, but God kept him from their hands, and in 1659, on (the) 27th of April, he died peaceably, and was buried in his own church of Kallusherry.

Q. 71. Why are the Syrians of Malabar called Pothen-koorkar, and such of those who have joined (such as have joined) with the Pope Palayakoorkar?

A. For eighty-six years all the Syrians were Papists, as Alleskes (de Menezes) made all the Syrians embrace Popery in the meeting at Vdyamperoor in 1599. But in 1685, when Mar Evanious came, those who forsook Popery by the instrumentality of that Bishop, and who at once newly adopted (re-adopted) Syrianism, were called Poothenkoorkar, (i.e.) New Partisans, and those who still clung to Popery after they had embraced it for eighty-six years olden (*sic*), were called Palay-akoorkar, (i.e.) Old Partisans.

Q. 72. How many different kinds of Syrians are there now?

A. The following six:—1st, Jacobite Syrians; 2nd, the Maronites, who once were Jacobites, but have lately joined the Pope; 3rd, the small company at Bagdad, who also have lately joined the Pope; 4th, the old Chaldees, who have adopted the Nestorian faith; 5th, the New Chaldees, who have embraced Popery; 6th, the Palayakoorkar, or such of the Syrians of Malabar as have adhered to Romanism.

Q. 73. Who is the present Bishop of the Syrian Churches in Malabar?

A. The present Bishop, who is appointed by the Patriarch, is Mar Coorilos Joyakim. But as his health was (has lately been) in a declining state, another Bishop, named Mar Devanasious, was (has) arrived in Malabar within a few days

before (within the last few days) from the Patriarch of
Antioch.

Q. 74. Who is Athanasious Matthew?

A. He is a native of Malabar, who, when a Deacon, had
been (was) expelled from the Syrian Church on account of his
great misconduct. He also learned in the Church Mission
School at Madras. And as he was prosecuting his studies
there, he was dismissed from that place too, owing to his bad
behaviour. Consequently he set out like a vagabond, and
reached the country Moosul in Turkish Arabia (*sic*), and imposed on the Syrian Christians there, (asserting) that he was
a Priest, and administered (administering) the Kooroobana (i.e.
the Korban, or Oblation, the Eucharist), the Holy Ceremony
which no Deacon has the power to administer. Thence he
went to the Patriarch of Antioch. He also forged and pro-
duced a letter to the Patriarch, as though it had been a general
recommendatory letter from the Syrian Churches, to the intent
that he should be ordained a Bishop. Having thus deceived
the Patriarch, and obtained the consecration of a Bishop, and
the name of Athanasious, he received a letter from the Patriarch, as to his consecration, to the Travancore Government,
and returned to Malabar in 1843.

Q. 75. What did the Patriarch do when he came to know
the truth of this?

A. The Patriarch deposed him from all his offices, and in his
room appointed the aforesaid Mar Coorilos Joachim, and Mar
Athanasious Stephanos as his assistant Bishop, whom he sent
to Malabar, together with letters to the Syrian Churches and
the Travancore Sircar, as to the deposition of Athanasious
Matthew, and the appointment of this (these) two persons in
his stead.

Q. 76. How do you know that the Travancore Sircar had
received the Patriarch's letter sent by these Bishops?

A. I can prove it by the following copy :—

(Copy.)

"No. 421 of 1849.

" To Major-General W. Cullen, Resident of Travancore.

" Sir,—I have the honour to acknowledge the receipt of your
letter of the 15th instant, No. 350, accompanied by a letter to His
Highness the Rajah, from the Patriarch of Antioch, brought by Mar
Athanasious Stephanos.

"The letter has been presented by me to His Highness, agreeably to your desire, and I will duly communicate to you His Highness' sentiments regarding the matters referred to when I am favoured with the same.

"I have the honour,

(Signed)   V. KRISHNO BOW (? Row), Dewan.

"Hassoor Catchery,
"Trevandrum, 29th March, 1849.

"A true copy.

"(Signed)   "W. CULLEN, Resident.

"To Mar Athanasious Stephanos, Cochin, for his information."

Q. 77. What were the proceedings of the Travancore Sircar after this with regard to this case?

A. The Government, without minding the aforesaid letter of the Patriarch, made a Proclamation favourable to the deposed Athanasious Matthew, which is as follows :—

"Translation of a Proclamation of His Highness the Maharajah of Travancore.

"No. 249.   Rayasum, dated 15th Carcadavem [July], 1027 [Malabar date].

"Whereas Mar Dionosious Metropolitan, residing at Cottayam, being old, and having abdicated his dignity; and as [we] appointed Mar Athanasious to that post as Metrapolitan, who is come with letters from Antioch, it is hereby notified that All Poothencoor Syrians belonging to the Malangara Edavaka [Malabar Diocese] should obey the aforesaid Mar Athanasious Metropolitan, and behave themselves as heretofore observed."

Q. 78. Where is the Assistant Mar Athanasious Stephanos now?

A. He left Malabar for England, and succeeded in getting an order from the Honorable Court of Directors, having complained for the same. But as his health was in a declining state, he has returned to the Patriarch.

(Copy.)

" Ecclesiastical Department.

" Extract from a Despatch from the Honourable Court of Directors,
" dated 13th May, No. 6 of 1857.

11 and 12, also para. 12 of letter dated 11th Nov. (No. 13) 1856. " Explanation of the Resident of Travancore with reference to the interference alleged to have been exercised by him in relation to the individuals claiming the office of Metropolitan of the Syrian Church in Travancore."	" 20. Lieutenant - General Cullen rests his refusal of permission to Mar Athanasius Stephanos to enter Travancore in 1849, on the practice of former Residents in analogous cases. We regret that our previously expressed desire for absolute non-interference was not strictly attended to, and that some ground was thus afforded for the allegations of Mar Athanasious Stephanos. It is stated that there is now a general acquiescence in the rule, as Metropolitan, of Mar Athanasius, the first appointed of the existing claimants to that dignity. This is a matter, the determination of which rests with the members of the Syrian Church alone, and it is for them to recognise or not the pretensions of any ecclesiastic who may be hereafter sent into the country by the Patriarch of Antioch. We desire that strict attention be paid to our instruction in this respect.	"Extract minutes Consultation, dated 14th July, 1857. " 6. Copy of this para. will be communicated to the Resident at Travancore for his information and guidance. That officer will pay particular attention to the wishes of the Honourable Court for the future."

" True Extracts.
" (Signed) E. MALTBY.
" Acting Chief Secretary.
" To the Resident of Travancore and Cochin.
" True copy.
" (Signed) W. CULLEN, Resident.
" Examined, I. A. WILSON."

Q. 79. Where is the above-mentioned Mar Coorilos Metropolitan now ?

A. He still remains in Malabar, and teaches such as come to him the Scriptures, and ordains priests and deacons. He also ordains a second time those priests and deacons who were (have been) ordained by Athanasious Matthew, on account of their going to him and confessing that they had done wrongfully in that they were ordained by him who was deposed by the Patriarch. But (I) suppose he [Coorilos] will go to (the) Patriarch, because another Metran is now reached from (the) Patriarch.

Q. 80. How does the aforesaid Athanasious Matthew go on now?

A. Because the Syrians of Malabar are poor and characteristically deficient of energy, he entices some by his winning speech, and frightens others with his threats. In this manner he travels through all the Churches, and takes all the Church properties by force, and ordains such of the people as are not approved of by the community; and he is taking to his house all the prices of the compound and paddy grounds belonged (belonging) to the Cottayam Seminary [College] in common (? with the Syrians), by selling them; thus creating dissensions and tumults in the churches, and ever continuing an enemy to the Patriarch and Syrian religion ᵃ.

Q. 81. Why do they fear his threats, and yield to his winning speech?

A. On account of the Proclamation mentioned in the answer to the 77th question, and a Circular Order of which the following is a copy:—

"Translation of a circular order, No. 2,455, dated the 3rd Coombum [February], 1038 [1863], addressed by the Dewan to the Tasildar of the different districts from Quilon to Paravoor, the Superintendents of Police at Trevandrum and Alwaye, and the Police Ameen at Paravom:—

"1. I have received a communication from Mar Athanasious, Syrian Metropolitan of Malabar, under date the 28th Thy last, in which he represents that one Mar Coorilos, assuming the office of a Metropolitan, is going about clandestinely from Church to Church, creating dissensions among the community, and that, joining those offenders who were excommunicated by the Church, he disturbs the peace, and perpetrates outrages, and therefore the Metropolitan finds it difficult to enforce the rules of the Church.

"2. There is no ground for the Sircar's interference in Religious Matters, yet it is necessary to adopt measures to prevent the commission of outrages.

"3. If there are any persons who are unwilling to follow the Church under Mar Athanasious, such persons may, after duly obtaining the permission of the Sircar, have Churches of their own

---

ᵃ The C.M.S ought to look well to their title, if, as seems to be implied, Athanasius is selling to them the share of the Syrians in lands left for their joint possession.—ED.

erected, and perform their religious duties in a peaceable manner. If there should be any among them who suppose that they have any lawful claim on the Church buildings under the authority of Mar Athanasious, they should have recourse to civil actions for the settlement of such claim. But it appears to me that if the Sircar permit persons to enter the Churches and act contrary to previous possession, it might lead to a breach of the peace, and the adequate punishment of those who might be so guilty. To obviate such consequences, it is my desire that my sentiments should be made known to both parties concerned, and that the Tasildars and others should clearly understand them, and act accordingly. If either the Metropolitan or any members of the community report that, notwithstanding these orders, any persons prove disobedient, and entering the Churches, act in a way contrary to previous possession, such persons should immediately be sent for, and tried by the police officers, and duly punished, if guilty, and the result reported.

"(Signed)   T. MADAVA ROW, Dewan."

Q. 82. What is to be considered about the Dewan (*i.e.* Prime Minister) of Travancore in enacting the above-mentioned Circular Order?

A. It is to be conjectured that T. Madava Row, the Dewan of Travancore, having believed that Athanasious being (is) a Bishop, will not utter falsehood; and he in future will enact another Circular Order contrary to the former, if he would happen to know the certainty of the fact. Besides, the Dewan is a person endowed with capacity and knowledge, and grateful to the inhabitants, especially to the Christians. After (Since) his appointment to the office, he has entirely abolished from the territories of Travancore the sin of bribery, and even the violence which the sub-officers are doing to the indigent inhabitants.

In a letter dated 17th Dec., 1866, the Author desires that the following Question and Answer may be added to the Tract:—

Q. Are there now any in Malabar who have adopted the Nestorian Faith?

A. No.

(Here follows)

A copy in Syriac (of) one of the letters of his Grace, the Right Rev. Father in God the Patriarch of Antioch, and

Primate of all Jacobite Syrians, about the dismissal of Athanasious Matthew [b] :—

(The translation of the same.)
Copy.

" In the Essential, Eternal Name, the necessary Essence that containeth all : Ignatius, Patriarch of the Apostolic Throne of Antioch,
who is Jacob the second the humble.

" May the Divine grace and heavenly blessing descend upon the
head of our spiritual son and right arm, the dear merchant and noble
foreigner, and head and great one, rich in spiritual things, and
treasurer of the King of kings [c], one zealous for the orthodox Faith,
and that presideth over spiritual riches; a wise man of science, and
a skilled philosopher ; constituter of Dominical Definitions and Apostolic Laws and Judgments; beloved of our Lord Jesus Christ ; to
wit, our beloved and dear son Maman of the land of Rhanni :—May
the Lord God prolong his life, and bless him, and his house, and all
that his right hand and his left hand collects; by the hand of the
prayers of Mary the Mother of God, and of all the Saints. Amen.

" And then, O my son, first of all our infirmity inquires concerning thy quality (= how thou art), and concerning the manner of thy
conversation in this afflicted and even tide-like time, while we ask
of God that thou mayest be in rest of soul and body. Amen.

" And repeatedly do we make known to thy love concerning the
matters of our beloved son, and the light of our eyes, Mar Koorillos
Joyakim, Metropolitan of your parts. When formerly there came
one whose name was Matthew, an impostor, from the land of India,
and brought a letter of Galtho as if from the mouth of all the people
of your land, and requesting by it of our Lord the Patriarch, the
pious Elias, that he would designate him Metropolitan of Malabar ;
he thus deceived our Father the Patriarch, and obtained by fraud
from him the divine gift, like Simon the Sorcerer ; and he returned
to your land with abundance of letters from the pious Patriarch to
the Rajahs and the Governours, and to all the people. And a little
afterwards our people, the priests and the religious and the chief
men of your land, reported to us that the accursed Matthew had
acted impiously, and was a heretic, and had changed his profession,
and had abolished the fasts and the customs and the Canons Apostolic, and had taught new customs at his own pleasure, and was
a heretic notable in heresies, and wished to mislead all our people,
such as would listen to him, and many had wandered after his vain
doctrine. And therefore the people sent and asked for a Metropolitan from hence, and exceedingly urged the compliance of our
Father the Patriarch Elias the holy. And he arose and consecrated

---

[b] The order of this title is here transposed, having been bungled by
the native writer.—ED.

[c] Perhaps a title of some Rajah.—ED.

for you his beloved secretary and treasurer Mar Koorillos Metropolitan, who is Joyakim the honoured. And he sent him to India
hour before hour, that he might expel the reprobate Matthew, and
keep from him all the flock of Mar Thomas, and might stand before
the face of the people, and administer the affairs of all the people,
and of the Churches that remain there to the Jacobite Syrians, and
likewise dispose the causes and administrations that happen before
the kings and sultans, that occur by reason of the neglect of the
governours. And he also anathematized the accursed Matthew, and
took care concerning him, that no man should agree with his frau-
dulent doctrine, or receive it, but should come to us. And again
he informed the Rajahs and the Governours concerning him, in order
that he should not be received by them in consequence of the letters
that he had given him for his reception. And especially he took
pains and care for the monks and for all the people, that instead of
him they should receive our beloved son Mar Koorillos, who is the
pious Joyakim the honoured, and taught that they should walk in
his footsteps in soul and in body.

" And now, in these days, our Lord the Patriarch, holy Elias,
died and went to his Lord. And all the people and the chosen
Fathers assembled, and took counsel in love with one another. And
by the will of God, and of all the assembly of the holy Fathers and
chief men and governours, the Patriarch designated me (or made me
Bishop) according to the custom of our Fathers that are blessed (=
dead). And we sit on the Throne of Peter which is fixed in the
monastery of Choorchoma, in the principality of the City Mardin :
and are invested with all the administration of our people without
and within ^d. And it was necessary that we should (?) also cause
to flow these weak words of blessing to thy true love; that thou
mayest acknowledge our administration, and mayest thyself write
to us concerning the goodness of thy spirit, and the mode of thy
conversation in all respects, that our heart also may be comforted
by thy suavity. This therefore do not thou forget. Be thou prepared to fulfil the commands of God, and of our spiritual son the
pious (= the Bishop) Mar Koorillos who is Joyakim the honoured :
for we have given to him the authority of the honourable head priesthood, even as our Lord the Patriarch gave it to him before, as thou
hast heard. And we have appointed him to bind and loose, as the
Apostolic Canons in the laws of our blessed Fathers command. And
let any one take heed that he do not secede. And thus again do we
anathematize the audacious Matthew, as our Father the blessed
Patriarch anathematized him. And no man shall in any wise have
authority to receive him, or to hear his words, and none shall pray
with him or consort with him on any ground whatsoever.

" Moreover I beg of you, O my beloved son, to assist this our son
Mar Koorillos, and to be prepared for all whatsoever he saith with-

^d Does this expression refer to exterior and interior jurisdiction ?—ED.

out hindrance, because he hath borne much distress for your sake. It is right that ye should know his worth : and do ye console him in his sojourning. And may the God of gods who filleth all, may He comfort you with His hope.

"And again, O my beloved son, we have heard that our spiritual son Mar Koorillos hath appointed thee fidejussor of our monastery of Choorchoma. We rejoice greatly : and now also confirm it that thou shalt be our fidejussor over all properties that we have, to wit, at (or for) our monastery of Choorchoma, in these blessed regions. And mayest thou ever stand in presence with our spiritual son Mar Koorillos, who is Joyakim the honoured. And from time to time write letters to us, and inform us of thy quality. And thus know. And may the grace of our Lord be with you all for ever and ever. Amen. Our Father which art in the heavens, et cetera.

"Written the 29th day in the month Ojar (May), in the year 1847 of Christ, from the city Mardin."

APPENDIX.

NOTE. The two letters that follow were sent to me (in their original form) in confirmation of the Author's statements regarding Athanasius Matthew. The writing in both is exceedingly small, that of the Patriarch's Letter being so diminutive that I have frequently used a glass to assist me in deciphering the characters. It is written on one side of a piece of paper measuring barely 5½ by 8¼ inches, of which fully a quarter is occupied by the superscription and the seal.

I regret that I could not give these seals; but a description of them may not be uninteresting.

That of the Metropolitan of Uraha is circular, 1¼ inches in diameter; the centre being occupied by a bearded figure in a vestment ornamented with six crosses: in the right hand he holds a cross-headed staff, and in the left a crozier with the crook turned outwards. Round the margin is the Legend— *Timotheos Metrō. of Urahi, who is Abraham* . . . [two curtailed words are illegible].

The seal of the Patriarch is a little more than 1½ inches in diameter. The centre is occupied by a bearded figure without the tonsure, the expression being severe and dignified. He wears a Vestment ornamented in front by a representation of glory rays, perhaps of the sun; but these are partly concealed by the Orrbo or Stole, which, after the Eastern fashion, comes down in a single piece in front. In the right hand is a cross, and two keys depend from it: and the left hand holds a crozier turned outwards. Around it is the Legend—*Ignatius Patr. of Antiochia, who is Elias* . . . [The rest seems to be a date]. Round this again are twelve heads, which may perhaps indicate the Apostolic College.

The lines of the Syriac are of very unequal lengths, being written according to the intended folds of the paper, and *obliquely* in the margins. The Persian king alluded to on p. 34 was Chosroes II., and the date A.D. 627—629.—ED.

The Metropolitan's Letter.

"In the Name of the Essential, Eternal, Necessary Essence That containeth all, Whom we glorify, Timotheus, Metropolitan of the Throne of Uraha (Edessa) and Keeper of the Tomb of St. Mar Ephraim, Who is Abraham of Jerusalem the humble.

[*Here is the Seal.*]

"May the tranquillity of the Essential Father, and the peace of the Only-begotten Son, Who is equal to His Father in Eternity, Who reconciled His Father with His creatures by His birth of the Virgin, and the overshadowing and illapsus of the Holy Ghost, Who is equal to the Father and to the Son in Eternity, Who descended upon and overshadowed the holy disciples in the upper room of Sion, and taught them wisdom and hidden mysteries—come and abide upon, and overshadow the heads of our dear and beloved sons, and of our beloved the priests and deacons, and on our Syrian
5 people, and on all the Churches of Malabar, and upon all true Christians who dwell in the cities of India the blessed. The blessing of the Lord God descend upon you, and upon your sons, and upon that which is conceived among you, by the prayers of the Mother of God, and of all the Saints and Saintesses, and of all the holy Martyrs. Amen.

"And again we ask your peace, and how your matters fare, because
10 your love is planted and settled upon the tables of our hearts. Yea, do we not diligently and continually bear you in prayer and supplication, especially at the hour of prayers, and at the Oblation of Korbans? And before the abodes of the Saints, Mar Peter and Mar Paul, and before the Tomb of the holy doctor of the Church of the Syrians, Mar Ephraim, and of all the Saints, we ask, we supplicate of God, that they may be assistants and helpers, and may He continually cause us to hear good reports from among you. And may the Lord God grant us to see and to receive one another. Amen."

In reply to their enquiry as to his health, he thanks God myriads and myriads of times that he is strong, and able to be a suppliant for the prolongation of their lives, &c.

He then speaks of the decay of Faith in India, and quoting S. John xxi. 18, laments that men had risen up from among them who had drawn them "away from the true Faith, like the *Throne* of Simeon, which led him whither he would not." They had "deserted the honour of Mary Mother of God, and the honour of the Cross," &c. Having quoted 1 Cor. i. 22, "For the Jews ask signs," &c., he proceeds to extol the glory of the holy Cross :—

34   "But glorious stands the name of the honourable and worshipful Cross. The great name was invoked for Heraclius, the king of the
35 Romans, who spoiled the king of the Persians, and gained authority over his cities, and put to flight his armies, and acquired great riches, and took the wood of the victorious Cross, which they had

taken when the king of the Beth Medians spoiled Jerusalem, and the
holy House, and all the Christian places. And when he reached Jerusalem, he would not enter into it excepting according to the custom
of (?) conquerors. Wherefore the sons of his city went to meet
him, and did him great honour, Patriarch and Governor, and both
great and small, when they saw the King carrying the saving wood
in his hands. Now he rode on his horse, and they went before him
till they reached Jerusalem. And the King's horse stood still at 40
the Gate of the City; and all men came (and) gathered round, and
they were not able to go up within the gates of the city. And all
men began to question, and the King also. After this the Patriarch
came to the King, and spoke to him; and the Patriarch said to
(him), 'O King, this is the gate through which our Lord our Saviour went, Who bore the Cross and bowed the head; and if thou 45
wilt enter thereby, descend from the horse, and put off the vest-
ments of thy royalty, and walk beneath the yoke of the life-giving
Cross, that thou mayest enter therein.' And when the King heard
the Patriarch's counsel, he put off his royal robes, and clothed himself in lowly raiment, and bowed his neck under the honourable
Cross, and in this guise went to the city, till he came to Golgotha,
and placed the Cross in the (?) honoured place. This is the holy
Cross which we venerate every day."

The Metropolitan continues the subject, addressing himself especially to the Presbyter Philipos "his dear and beloved Brother,"
and praying God to give him—or as he puts it "to my littleness"—
" mouth and wisdom to explain from the Divine Scriptures concerning these things."

" If thou inquire, O man, denying that the Cross is honourable
above all; we also say to your love as said the Prophet, Cursed is
he that is crucified on a tree. Formerly, if any sinner was guilty
of death, they used to crucify him on a cross, and did not leave his
corpse on the tree, but used to bury him the same day, because he
that was lifted up on a tree was accursed of God. None were crucified but blasphemers and worshippers of idols. Therefore after- 60
wards when our Lord Jesus Christ, the Saviour of the worlds, was
lifted up upon it, He sanctified it by His precious blood, and en-
nobled it in the person of His Godhead. And the tree of shame
was changed and became glorious: and the curse also became
a blessing: and the Stevros (σταυρός, cross) was honoured above
everything that is on earth; as the Apostle Paul testifies to the
Corinthians the first, saying, The Jews ask signs and the Gentiles
seek for wisdom; but we preach Christ crucified, a snare to the
Jews, and to the Gentiles foolishness; to them that are called,
Jews and Gentiles, Christ is both the power of God and the wisdom
of God. And again, by the Cross was revealed the love of God 65
towards us. For it was not of necessity that Christ came down
from the bosom of His Father and suffered; but of His own will

He took our nature and clothed Himself with our body, and took on Him the Cross for our redemption. And truly the Cross is the Wisdom of God, because by the Cross was manifested the power of God. And martyrs testified concerning His (its) Name, and powers and prodigies were made known by them. As said the Golden mouth (i.e. St. Chrysostom), The Cross is the hope of the faithful: The Cross is the resurrection of the dead: The Cross opposeth devils: The Cross is the teacher and preceptor of the unskilful:
70 The Cross is the hope of them that are without hope: The Cross is the conductor of them that are girded for journies: The Cross is a Father of Orphans, and a Guardian of Widows: The Cross is a light to them that sit in darkness and in the shadow of death: The Cross is an honour to Kings: The Cross is the Guardian of Monasteries, and the illustrator of Monks and Virgins: The Cross is the joy of priests and the foundation of Churches: The Cross is strength to the weak, and healing to the sick, and nourishment to the hungry. Paul the Apostle saith, I have no glory except in the Cross of Christ; for the world is crucified unto me, and I unto the world. . . . . .

"Again we ? praise [the word is not clearly legible; the sense would seem to require *admonish*] you concerning the honour of Mary the Mother of God, the Mother of true Christians, and Mistress of Angels. Especially is it fitting for us to honour her more than all' the Saints and Apostles and Martyrs; and to acknowledge the
85 honour of the Saints; as it is written in the holy and worshipful Gospel in Matthew, He that receiveth you receiveth Me, &c. . . .

"And again we make known unto you, even 1 Timotheos Metran*, Abraham of Jerusalem, least among Bishops, and a servant
90 of the Tomb of Mar Ephraim, the Doctor of the Churches of the Syrians that is in the place strong in God, Euraha blessed herein, that all doctors after him have taught both peoples and nations by his sweet doctrines and satiating sermons, whose bones give voices from his tomb and say, My bones shall cry out from the sepulchre that the Virgin bare God, and the rest.

"Again, when your letter reached us by the hands of our spiritual son Nelomch Allah Ozor Barwaaya the Syrian, we both read it and understood it, wherein is written concerning the doings (a word or words illegible here) by the hands of the Metran Matthew and
95 Abraham who is not a Presbyter, et cetera. They have both seduced you from the true faith, and have deserted the honour of Mary the Mother of God, and the honour of the holy Martyrs, and (of) the worshipful Cross, and the remembrance of the dead, et cetera. And they have abolished the genuflections, and the Remembrance of our Lord and our God from the order of the Corbano, and they have blotted out the Canon of the Saints from the Book of Prayers, and the Faith is blotted out from blessed Malabar, and some of our sons

---

* I suspect this is a contracted form of the word Metropolitan.

have been deceived and have gone after the corrupters, and have left the true Faith, and have gone after that which is nothing.

"Again, holy Cyril, Patriarch of Alexandria, (gives) instruction concerning the advantage that is (derived) from the Oblation for the dead and for the living. It happened then, in his time, that holy 100 Cyril was sailing on the sea on a certain day, and came to an island, and found on it a man who was kept there, who, when he saw them, begged of them that he might be carried in the ship and go to his own place. The Saint then asked him, What is the reason that you stand here? He then answered him, I was sailing for merchandise in a ship, and the ship sunk, and the men that were in it were drowned, and I was saved on one of the planks, and was brought to this place. The holy Cyril then asked him, How many years hast 105 thou been in this place? And he said, Three years, more or less. The Saint said to him, With what hast thou been nourished? He said to him, From Sabbath to Sabbath there came (?) an abundance (or perhaps, a Victim) of bread, and therewith have I been nourished, and it preserved my life to me all the week. He sailed and was brought to his place, and came to his masters seeking his house. When it was so that his wife heard of the sinking of the ship, she gave up all hope, as over the dead, and her employment every week 110 by week (was that) she made Oblation for him. And when he came himself, and related all the history, all men perceived that it was by the Oblation that had been made for him, that he had also himself been assisted when there. And this is consoling to those (who) value Corbanos for their dead and also for their friends. Ye see, O my brothers and beloved, how profitable is the Corbano to those that are 115 gone. Thus do ye as ye see from the holy Fathers and from the Orthodox Doctors. Amen.

"When the message came by the hands of our beloved and dear 120 son, Nelomch Allah Ozor the Syrian, and we had read it, we also wept, and our tears ran down our face, and great was the anguish of our heart. We wept: day and night we had no comfort. Come, O thou prophet Jeremiah, weep this day with us, as thou didst weep over Jerusalem! Come thou father of lamentations, weep over the great city Malabar, and over the other cities of India and them that dwell in them, our Syrian people! How is the fine gold become 125 dim, and the beautiful colour changed! Forasmuch as the Metran Matthew hath invaded you like a pernicious wolf, and an owl that cries in the wilderness, ye must not listen to him, nor join yourselves to him, nor go after him; but ye must fly from him, as a lamb flies from a wolf! This bold fellow hath undone his soul and body. Impudently came he to our Lord Mar Ignatius the Patriarch, who holds the Apostolic Throne, who is Elias the honoured—the Lord God exalt his throne! This fellow came to our Lord, representing himself to 130 be one of our people, and he deceived our Lord the Patriarch, and rapaciously obtained from him the High Priesthood. And our Lord the Patriarch was holy and sincere and simple and straightforward: he did not know the deceit of this corrupter. He is a serpent,

[Then four words I cannot make sense of.] If thou nourishest a serpent, thou wilt have no advantage therefrom, but bites only. And
135 ye, stand ye on the Foundation of Peter, and the true and Orthodox Faith, and on the three holy Synods. Change nothing from the Customs of the holy Fathers, and labour and toil in the vineyard of Christ our Lord, and walk in the paths of the holy Fathers, those that are fitting for us, and do not lead us away from anything that they have commanded us, who have gone before and are passed away.
140 And ye, may ye be rich in the gifts of God. Every one that is not rich in God is poor; and he that is rich in God is higher than kings and governours of the earth, and very rich.

"Thus know ye: and from us abundance of blessing and peace (be) upon priests and deacons, and upon the princes of our people, upon great and small, and upon men and women, and upon boys and girls, and upon virgin men and virgin women. May the blessing of God, which rested on the table of our Father Abraham, rest on your
145 houses, and on your children, and on all that you have. Amen.

"If you ask from Edessa to Brujo, it is a road of five days. And when our letter comes to your hands, read it, and hasten answering words, for our eyes are on the way. If ye write to us, hither may (the letter) come to the city Uraha, to the holy Church of Mar Peter and Paul.

"And it is delivered by the hands of the Metran Abraham of Jerusalem the humble.

"Our Father who art in the heavens, and the rest."

In a vacant corner near line 40 is the date as below:—

"It was poured forth 13 in the month Tisrin, the year 2156 of the Greeks." (i.e. A.D. 1845.)

There is something additional of little importance, and four stanzas that I cannot translate, on the back.

The Patriarch's Letter.

"In the Name of the Essential, Eternal, Necessary Essence That containeth all, Ignatius, Patriarch of the Apostolic Throne of Antioch, who is Elias II. the humble.

[*Here is the Seal.*]

"Ignatius the humble, by the grace of God the Father, and the will of the Only-begotten Son, our Lord and our God, and our Saviour Jesus Christ, and the communion and illapsus of the Holy Ghost, Patriarch of Antioch the opulent, and the Place of the rivers (Mesopotamia), and Syria, with all the East, the Mother of Light; Peace. To my true son and branch that standeth upright in the discipline of the Truth, and (is) diligent and watchful in chaste conversation (conduct) to the confirmation of the orthodox

Faith, the honoured monk Mar Dionysius, blessed old man (two 5
words here uncertainly legible). May the Lord preserve him from
all hurtful things that afflict soul and body, and honour his blessed
old age, and make him seasoning salt to insipid faith, and a per-
former and partaker in the Divine Mysteries, and sound and pleasant
to them that are pleasing to God, by the hand of the prayers of Mary
the Mother of God, and all the elect and saints. Yea and Amen.
And after repetition of peace, with no brief prayer and supplication, 10
then my weakness asks concerning your quality in this transitory
and dissolving life, and concerning your conversation in these times
when we ask that in verity ye may be diligent and zealous in the
true faith, and further, firm in the hope that is not ashamed
(the hope) of the new world that is coming for the refreshment of
the diligent, and the reward of the righteous, and in words and
deeds careful for good works, a good example to such as behold,
a light to the dark, and a rebuke to the vile and indolent.
"And mayest thou be a Governour to thy brethren in the love
and concord of the Spirit, that they may know thee a true disciple 15
of the lively Gospel of our Saviour, who said, Herein shall every
man know that ye are My disciples, when ye love one another; and
hereby gave us an example, that we should be bound with one
another in Divine Love, and be far removed from anger and all
envy, and not reproach one another, lest one be doubly quarrelsome
with us. Herein hath He strongly cautioned us, that if we do not
love one another, He receiveth us not as disciples in His service,
yea, even though we please him in all other things; as the Divine
Apostle testified, when he said, Although I do all good things in
what things soever, without abundance of charity I have no ad- 20
vantage. And if I deliver my body to be burned, and if all I have
I make to feed the poor, and if I keep all the law and the rest of
the commandments, and charity be not in me, I profit nothing, and
I am nothing, yea, though I remove the mountain. Now from
hence it is certain that without charity towards God and towards
the neighbour, we do not in any wise acquire a good name. And
now we will pray to our Lord, though we are unworthy, that He
may enable you to keep his commandments in all fear of God, and
(that) ye may be to Him good servants and sons of obedience. Yea
and Amen.
And further, there hath come to us a letter from your love, and 25
one from my beloved son and light of my eyes, Mar Koorillos
Joyakim the honoured, Metropolitan of India, Land of Malabar
the blessed: and it is known to us that, when this beloved son
arrived among you, ye went forth to meet him with joy and praise,
and he was received with abundance and numbers, when he con-
fessed the true love that ye beheld with him. And we have been
informed that, lo, ye sit with one another, as it is right for true
brethren. And (when) we heard this, there was added to us glad-
ness of heart that thou wast subject in Divine love with my son,
whom I sent unto you. And again now I desire that ye may in

30 truth love one auother, that God may direct your way. And know
that this my son Mar Koorillos Metropolitan Joyakim, hath made
mention of his (?) desolation, not without care. Nevertheless do
thou stand with him, with the houour that is meet, in all his
matters, because he is very dear to me, and all that he commands
from us is the same that I have signified by his hand for all neces-
sities of your uses. And now know ye that whosoever receiveth
him receiveth us; and whosoever sets him at naught aud despiseth
him, despiseth us. Aud especially I pray you to be in concord one
with another, and to drive out the accursed and anathematized
Matthew from all the land of Malabar, if possible. And behold
35 I have written letters regarding him to the Rajahs who rule over
you. Do ye also be girded about, and loose not your hand amoug
your people. And we also in very truth stand iu supplication before
the living God for you, that ye may perfect a good contest and also
receive a crown that fadeth not. Be ye observant and zealous; and
the grace of our Lord be with you. Amen.

　　　　　　　" 2 in the month
　　　　　　　　　written
　　　　　　Adar, the year 1847 of Christ.
40　　" And agaiu I have a longing to see you before I die. I hear, however, that ye are old, aud there remaineth not in you the power to
come. And we also, all weak, would cause (you) to uuderstand
45 this, that, behold, I am bent with age, and am not able to come to
you. Nevertheless, by the power of God we are perpetually present
in spirit, inasmuch as we do not cease to be in prayer for you. And
50 I trust in God that He will be a good Shepherd to you, and a tender
Father, and will lead you on. And this is the sum of our request
to your true love, that ye would honour my beloved sou whom we
55 have sent unto you, by the example of the Apostle Thomas, according to the custom of the Fathers before (us), oue after another.
Receive his words, and obey him as ourselves, and as a Father and
60 true Shepherd. Aud comfort him much because the place is strange.
Aud kuow that it is meet that he should have greatness of honour
at your hands, because he hath despised kindred aud family, iu sad-
65 ness, and hath raised himself up for your sake. Whereas we have
urged many Fathers, truly brethren, to go uuto you, aud uot oue
70 hath disposed himself to go abroad like him : and he hath done all
for your love to the glory of the living God. And now there are
prepared with him before the Kings, and the Governour aud his
assistants, in all that happens concerning him, whether from the
75 accursed Matthew, or whether from the tenants of the land, or
whether from the accusations of euemies : they are with him prepared without prolonged delay, so that he may not be molested in
80 anything : for the circumspect are very dear to me. And may the
help of God assist you. Amen.
　　" And Our Father which art in the heaveus," &c.

www.ingramcontent.com/pod-product-compliance
Lightning Source LLC
Chambersburg PA
CBHW021234260626
47172CB00002B/758